RETURN TO MOUNT ATHOS

FATHER SPYRIDON BAILEY

Also by Father Spyridon:
Journey To Mount Athos
The Ancient Path
Trampling Down Death By Death
Fire On The Lips
Podvig
Come And See

RETURN TO MOUNT ATHOS

FATHER SPYRIDON BAILEY

FaR

Published in 2018 by FeedARead.com Publishing
Financed by the Arts Council of Great Britain.

A CIP catalogue record for this title is available
from the British Library.

Foreword by Father Ioakeim Oureilidis

A visit to Mount Athos, more commonly known as the Holy Mountain (and as the dowry that humanity offered to Holy Mary as the Bride of God), the Garden of Holy Mary, a gift from fallen humanity to the elevated woman, is a wish and a dream of almost every Orthodox Christian. The Theotokos is the absolute woman and the one who reversed human history in its relation with God, since Adam and Eve first lost the Garden that God gave to humanity,

This pilgrimage is talked about as a life changing experience which leaves a permanent stamp of hope and relief in one's faith and cleanses our view towards the truths of Christian practice. It is a revelation which communicates the most precious values of prayer and uncovers aspects of spirituality which one does not have the opportunity and the frame of mind to comprehend in the secular way of living with its frantic pace and the adversities that one has to face. Many people say that to the soul, this pilgrimage is equal to the relief and satisfaction that a thirsty hiker in the desert experiences at the view of a well or a spring.

Fr. Spyridon Bailey, a gifted writer, a devout and assiduous worker in the vineyard of the Lord in the Biblical Archdiocese of Thyateira and Great Britain, offers us an insight to his second visit to the Holy Mountain, which as he says, was something that he longed for.

Through his unfussy, dynamic narrations and lively descriptions he offers comprehensive and useful insight to the preparations for the journey, the difficulties he came up against, the solutions that were offered and the people that he met on his journey. They all seem to be working small and continuous miracles as the problems seem to beg to be solved and help is at hand without Fr. Spyridon and his fearless son being in a position to seek for it in any other way than through prayer and faith.

The inviting narratives in the book prove to be educational for anyone who would like to visit the Holy Mountain as it offers abundant information on the preparation, the hurdles, the difficulties and the setbacks in the timetable that every pilgrim should allow himself to experience, as this trip will, in retrospect, prove that it involves a factor that no man can initially anticipate, and this is no other than the providence of her grace for everyone that decides to visit her earthly garden.

The writer offers a vivid description of the Holy Mountain's landscapes, sounds and atmosphere that are inviting to someone who would like to visit it and brings to mind pictures, feelings and smells to the people who have been there before and they re-live the experience and feel that they are walking side by side with Fr. Spyridon and his son Joseph in their tour on Mount Athos. He also offers an insight to the local culture of Thessaloniki, which is the city where the journey to the Holy Mountain starts for most of the pilgrims and the mind frame that people who visit the Mount develop due to the pilgrimage which seems to revamp them in faith and the practice of the divine wish. He refers to the way that the priest is seen and respected in the area and how hospitality and respect for a foreigner materializes in the legendary Greek hospitality.

The stay on the mountain journeys us through the inexpressible revelations of the liturgical life of mount Athos by deploying the feelings and the experiences of the writer as he participates in them and reveals in subtle phrasing but powerful sequence the might of prayer and the sacramental and apocalyptic nature of worship.

The spiritual life both Fr Spyridon and Joseph, his son, experience is not limited to the church building itself, but extends to every step, picture and discussion they have with some elder monks on the mountain. Amazingly, Fr Spyridon makes a wise approach to these consultations and does not attempt to interpret the messages that he receives or the rather "peculiar" and "special" vocabulary and form of expression of the language of Mount Athos. Instead, he manages through the transcription of the actual words to let the reader discover the wealth, the diversity and the richness of the language of the fathers of the Holy Mount.

Indeed, the language of the fathers of the Holy Mountain is rich in metaphors, personifications and allegory and if one has not got the wealth of experiencing the faith, it demands a lot of effort in terms of biblical study and experience in faith for one to be able to get an insight into the meaning and the ampleness of the words, let alone comprehend the depth of the meaning and the multitude of the theological messages emitted that have a practical value in our everyday life: the discussions with the fathers on the Holy Mount is a cornucopia of messages on life in Christ. The most capable and highly talented writer manages to make the conversations accessible to the reader refraining from giving rise to any bias in what has been heard but invites the reader to participate in the discussion as a listener and try to be part of the experience. He keeps an uncomplicated narration using articulate and accurate wording which features the level and the background of his encounter with the monks and the other visitors and pilgrims, in order to help the reader sense and live rather than strictly direct him/her towards receiving an unfairly lopsided view of theological and ethical meanings.

It is not clear to me whether I should see this book as merely narrating one's experience or a writing of linguistic beauty. It seems that together with all the above this book is primarily a spiritual invitation through this paper object, this book, that our Holy Mary, our Panagia, making good use of Fr Spyridon's skills and talents, extends to us all to visit her earthly home, the Holy Mountain in order to be rejuvenated through faith and communication with the praying fathers and her grace. I opt for this explanation and I praise Fr. Spyridon for his effort and I commend him on the result. Now, if one prefers to see this book as merely a narrative or a travelling experience I am sure that they will be gratified and they will be able to see the Orthodox faith and the world around it with a clear vision and from a new and loving perspective.

Introduction

From the first time I read about Mount Athos in the late 1980s I felt its pull. But more than the history, its countless saints, or its unique position within Orthodox spirituality, it was the photographs that I kept coming back to. I would look at those bearded faces and see in them something I couldn't explain, but about which I knew I had to learn more. They were faces sculpted by hours of prayer and material hardship, and in the cracked skin and sunken cheeks there was a joy that nothing in this world could create. Most Greek men will have been taken at some point on pilgrimage when they were young. But today you are as likely to meet a Russian, Australian or Romanian pilgrim as you are a native of Greece. Just as the man who pursues pleasure will be drawn to bars and places of worldly sensation, so those who have tasted even a little of the spiritual sweetness of God's presence will seek the peninsula where He is found in abundance.

It was not until 2013 that I finally made my first trip to the Holy Mountain, a trip that exceeded all of my expectations. Only by making the trip was I able to recognise how many fantasies I had developed about Athos, and the reality that replaced them was greater than anything I could have imagined. Hoping simply to meet with these other-worldly faces, instead I found myself drawn deeper into the reality of God's presence. All the photographs in the world cannot communicate the real nature and purpose of Athos, it is like trying to imagine the taste of food by reading recipe books. The experience of prayer, even as a visitor for just a few days, is to enter a living tradition that has been unbroken for over a thousand years. The monks exist in both this world and the world to come, their lives are spent at the meeting of earth and Heaven. And the place of this meeting is in the prayerful heart; it is here that Christ dwells with an intimacy unequalled by any human relationship. It is a union which every person is created for, it is in our nature to need it. On Athos every aspect of life is organised to make this meeting of man and God possible; through the centuries the monks have found the simple path that enables sinful creatures to be transformed into God's sons. And even a brief encounter with this reality can be life changing. If we are able to let go of the unnecessary burdens we bring with us, pilgrims can have their feet turned to at least find something of this simple path. We return to the world changed, and there is the possibility of allowing the impact of this change to radiate out into our lives like the ripples in a pond. God gives to each of us different blessings according to His infinite wisdom, and if we respond then the blessing can be for our families, friends and neighbours too. Athos permits us to carry spiritual treasures to a world that is so often attempting to get by in utter poverty. So long as we do not keep this wealth to ourselves, the generosity of the monks may combine with their prayers to transform the whole world. There are many who believe that without the continuous prayers of Orthodox monastics there could be no life of faith for any of us. At every moment we know that somewhere, perhaps in a forest, in a cave on a rocky outcrop hanging over the sea, or gathered in their churches, the monks are praying that God will allow us more time to repent. The hours and days of our lives are sustained by their prayer: though they have chosen to remove themselves from the activities of worldly life, they carry us with them.

Chapter 1

It had been three years since I had first visited Mount Athos and thoughts of returning began to present themselves at unexpected times. I had no great plan of when I would make another pilgrimage to the Holy Mountain, but the hope that I would be able to go back one day was never far from my mind. As the idea of returning began to present itself more frequently, I started to assess the practicalities of whether the time was right. I was working as a teacher, which meant that I could only travel during school holidays, and the hike in the prices of airline tickets outside of term time meant I would struggle to find the money. But the memories from my first trip were powerful, and the more I thought about sitting with the monks in their cells and the night-long services filled with unearthly beauty, the stronger my desire to return grew.

But there was a problem. My wife hadn't had a holiday for a few years, and she was in need of a break. I knew it would be selfish to suggest I use what little spare cash we had to go off alone while she sat at home waiting for me to return. So I didn't mention it, knowing it wasn't the right time. Or at least, that's what I thought. The school I was teaching at was struggling to maintain its necessary number of students, and the management decided to make teachers redundant. When it was confirmed that I would be leaving, I discovered my twelve years at the school had built up a decent redundancy package: suddenly Athos was a possibility. While friends offered their concern for my sudden lack of employment, I secretly rejoiced at the opportunity God seemed to be offering.

I broached the subject carefully, but to my surprise my wife showed as much enthusiasm for my trip as I was feeling, partly because I wanted to take one of my sons with me (the other was working). My first pilgrimage to Athos had been alone, and having my twenty-one year old son along would make this second trip a different kind of experience. Joseph had listened to stories from my first trip many times, and when asked whether he would like to go he jumped at the chance. Once it was decided, the realisation that I was really going back began to sink in, and my days took on a sense of anticipation that made everything feel as though it was leading to this event ahead. My sense of time began to shape itself into the distance between the now I was in and the moment when I would step off the ferry onto the peninsula once more.

Being an Orthodox priest meant receiving permission to stay at the monasteries would be reasonably straight forward, but it also meant I needed to first gain written authorisation from the Ecumenical Patriarch in Turkey. By December I was coming to the end of my teaching and so wrote to my Archbishop asking for his blessing for the trip. Within a week I received a letter from him giving me permission to go, and an assurance that he had written to the Patriarch on my behalf. I stashed the letter away in a safe place and got on with celebrating Christmas. By January I had heard nothing, and knew I couldn't make any further arrangements until I had the necessary documents. I tried to be patient but also wanted to start making concrete plans. The weeks passed and I heard nothing more, and I began to get nervous as I was hoping to make the trip before Pascha. Eventually we were preparing to enter Great Lent and I was still without the Patriarch's letter. I emailed the Archbishop's office and was assured that they would look in to it. Within twenty four hours they had made the necessary calls and I was informed that the letter was on its way.

Immediately I called the Athos Pilgrim's Office to arrange for our permits that would gain us entry into Athos. My previous experience dealing with them had been one of utter frustration. Depending on who I spoke to I was given different information, and right up to the day I was meant to be entering Athos I had expected to find an error had been made. But this time couldn't have been more different. From the very first call a date was set and I was assured that all would run smoothly. I sent copies of our passports and of the Archbishop's letter by email (just three years earlier it had been done by fax machine) and so I turned to contacting the monasteries.

On my first pilgrimage I had studied maps of Mount Athos and chosen monasteries I felt I could reach by foot. I was to discover that what looked like short distances on paper required many hours of walking in Greek August sunshine to cover. This time I made enquiries about the ferries that run along the coastline and decided we would visit monasteries further apart. I looked at the layout along the coast and wrote a few possible names down. I wanted to visit places I hadn't previously been to, and there were some sketes that appealed to me. However, above all else I wanted to return to the Monastery of St. Gregoriou. On my first pilgrimage I had received a generous welcome everywhere I had gone, but at Gregoriou Monastery I had met a monk who had given me hours of his time in private conversation. My hope was to introduce Joseph to him in the hope of exposing him to a little of the monastic wisdom from which I had benefitted.

I found the map I had downloaded three years before from the "Friends of Mount Athos" website and began to survey my options. As I was confident about finding my way to Ouranoupolis and entering Athos from the western side I discounted venturing round to the other side of the peninsula. Further on down the coast from Gregoriou were two monasteries I had not previously visited and so I decided to plan our trip around these three. But Lent had begun, and my previous experience of finding a monk at the end of each telephone call was not to be repeated. I rang at as many different times in the morning as I could (all pilgrim guides advise not to call after lunch) but got nothing. Eventually I reached the Monastery Ossiou Gregoriou, but was disheartened to be told that on the day I was hoping to visit the monastery it was fully booked. I asked for other days and managed to find a date where they could accommodate us. At least we had one monastery for certain. For the best part of two weeks I persisted with telephone calls and continued to listen to the unanswered ringing. Feeling a little concerned I looked to the map once more and decided to try the two monasteries I had also previously visited, Simona Petras and Xiropotamou. I looked their numbers up but once more couldn't get through. Having assured my son that the trip was happening I felt a little discouraged and wondered if it was God's will for us not to go. But then, in the space of two days, my calls were answered, Simona Petras was also fully booked but at least Xiropotamou had space. Having given up on my original plan I looked further back along the peninsula coastline and decided to try the Russian monastery of Saint Panteleimon. I found an email address and made my request. The following day I was delighted to receive a booking form which I immediately returned; we had our monasteries. It would mean landing on the peninsula before the ferry reached the small port of Daphne where most pilgrims enter Athos. Looking at the map I estimated it would take just a couple of hours to walk along the coast to reach the port after our stay at Panteleimon, and we could then catch one of the smaller ferries to Gregoriou.

My plan was for us to land in Thessalonica and take a taxi to the bus station where we could catch a bus to Ouranoupolis from where the ferries depart for the Holy Mountain. As I began booking hotels I received an email from an English priest who had heard about our trip and was himself visiting Athos in the same week. He had the use of an apartment in Thessalonica for a couple of weeks and kindly offered us its use for the two days after we would leave Athos. This meant we would be able to visit some of the churches in the city, and though it was likely to become something of a holiday rather than a pilgrimage, it would mean we could visit the relics of Saint Gregory Palamas. When Joseph discovered we would have extra time he immediately suggested we visit the Monastery of Saint John the Theologian, situated not far from Thessalonica, where Saint Paisios is buried. I would have liked to visit him too, but wondered if we would have time. I managed to assure Joseph we would make a decision about it when we were in Greece, but secretly suspected it would be unlikely to happen. After our stay at the apartment I had a room booked at the Hotel Avalon which is close to the airport and provides a free taxi service. On paper it all looked straight forward, and whereas I had headed out last time unsure if my limited language skills was going to be a problem, this time I had no such anxieties. Having made the trip once I knew there were enough people who spoke English for everything to go smoothly; and furthermore I had been practicing and was keen to try out my newly acquired Greek.

On my previous trip I had had a number of personal questions I hoped to have answered. This time was no different, there were some theological issues I couldn't resolve, and I hoped to hear the Athonite perspective to help put them to rest. I also encouraged Joseph to think about anything he might want to raise.

The day of our departure arrived and my wife waved us off at the railway station. In order to get from Herefordshire to London we would have a day of travelling: it was quicker to fly from London to Greece than to travel half the length of England. But we were in good spirits on the train, and the hours passed quickly. The train pulled into Gatwick and we grabbed our bags. As we stepped out onto the platform we entered the crowd heading towards the escalator. We only had a small bag each, nothing more than we could carry between monasteries, and easily found our way onto the ascending stairs. At the top of the escalator we were confronted with the bright artificial lighting of an international airport, and the sense of everyone being on route to somewhere else. The enclosed open space buzzed with the excited energy of people about to fly. Cases on wheels rattled along behind families in a rush, while other groups sat drinking or staring out at the scene as they waited for the time to pass. There was a mixture of anticipation and nervousness in the faces around us, the prospect of boarding an aeroplane was clearly having an effect on everyone.

I had a slight sense of familiarity, "I think we need to head that way." I pointed past a coffee stand, and Joseph nodded. As we passed them few people gave me a second glance dressed in my black; airports give enough of a sense of other places for any signs of different cultures to become ordinary.

We spotted a sign proclaiming the name of our hotel over a set of lift doors, and waited for the elevator to arrive. We rode it down a single floor and the doors opened to the silence of a reception area that felt surreal after the noise and busyness above us. The young man behind the desk smiled as he looked up at us.

"Hello, I have a room booked for Bailey," I said.

He prodded at his keyboard while looking at his computer screen. "I am sorry, your booking in time is not for another two hours." A wave of disappointment passed over me. Had I been alone I would have wandered off to kill time over a coffee, but having brought my son down into London I felt the need to find a space for us to settle.

"Is there no way we can book in early?"

"Yes," he smiled again, "we have an early booking option for an additional ten pounds."

Without a moment's hesitation I reached into my pocket, "That'll be great," I said.

The hotel was designed to look like a space station, something they had succeeded in pulling off. The rooms had signs declaring which number capsule they were, and along the corridor curved plastic archways completed the sense of a non-terrestrial environment. We opened our electronic door and stepped into a futuristic room that was unlike anything we had seen elsewhere. Dumping our bags beside the beds we stretched out and kicked off our shoes. "I'm knackered," Joseph said half to himself, "but it's good to stop moving."

"We'll go back up and get some food later," I assured him, "why don't you have a shower?"

Beside my bed was a perspex wall with a sliding door that separated the main area from the toilet and shower room. He rolled his head over and calculated whether the relief of hot water was worth the cost in effort it would take to get to his feet. "Yea, I think I will." He slid his legs over the side of the bed and disappeared behind the plastic wall. I turned onto my side to give him some privacy, and despite my physical tiredness found my mind racing. This time tomorrow we would be able to see Mount Athos from the beach of Ouranoupolis. I thought about Joseph and how different his life was from what mine had been at his age. To be travelling to Athos in his early twenties gave him a huge head start on anything I had had. At that age I was still fumbling around with basic ideas of who God is and where the Church was to be found. But at twenty-four I had met a monk from Athos, a meeting which had redirected my whole life. It was an encounter which opened up to me a world of prayer which until that point I had never imagined could exist.

Not only had Joseph already had conversations with monastics, but here he was about to travel into the heartland of Orthodox spirituality. My prayer was that we would both be blessed through our pilgrimage, but my greatest longing was that through whatever experiences he was about to have God would bless Joseph here at the beginning of his adult life.

Rejuvenated by his shower he persuaded me to go watch the aeroplanes. We headed up into the noise once more and followed the sign posts until we were looking out of a long window at the jets. Watching a few take off and land safely settled my nerves, it was reassuring to see how frequently it happened, and how unspectacular it was. We wandered down to the restaurants and ate some overpriced food before finally heading back to the hotel. Once we were safely settled in we lay out on the beds, flicking through the news channels on the television hanging on the wall opposite us. Without announcing it, Joseph rolled over to sleep. I muted the TV and rummaged around in my bag for my alarm clock. Not having bags to check in, and having already printed off our boarding passes, we didn't need to be at the departure gate until 6-30am. I set the alarm for an hour earlier, and then checked twice that the switch was on before finally convincing myself that we wouldn't miss our flight. Tired as I was, I lay in the dark for a long time before sleeping. I ran my prayer rope though my fingers and tried to bring my mind back to the presence of God. But I was too aware of my surroundings, too distracted by my thoughts, and with little success in what was important, I eventually fell into sleep.

Chapter 2

Waking to an early alarm clock can evoke all kinds of feelings, but as I was yanked from sleep by the high pitched call I immediately felt excitement at the prospect of what the day would bring. I lay still for about thirty seconds, listening for movements from Joseph, but there in the darkness his breathing was still regular and uninterrupted. I lifted myself to the edge of the bed and pressed my feet down into the carpet. As they made contact I imagined how far from the earth they would be in a few hours, and a wave of anxiety passed over me. I brushed the nerves away as best I could, and quietly began to pray. The words I had learned silently shaped my lips, and I knew that whatever God willed would happen.

I stood and switched on the lighting behind the plastic wall so that a soft light radiated out across our beds.

"Joe, it's time to get up."

From beneath his quilt I heard "Yea, in a minute."

I splashed cold water into my face and beard and caught sight of myself in the mirror. Just three years ago my hair had been black, but now at least half my beard was grey, which gave me the appearance of an older man. It made me aware of how quickly time was passing, and with this came a powerful sense of mortality. At least we were heading to Athos, we were using whatever little time we had left to draw closer to God.

By the time I returned to the bedroom Joseph was up and dressed, waiting to use the sink. While he washed I stuffed my belongings back into my bag and finally pulled on my rasso. We had brought so little that within ten minutes we were done and heading along the half-lit corridor back to reception. A different young man now sat behind the desk and took our electronic key from us with as much courtesy as he could muster through his lack of sleep. We paid and walked over to the lift doors which opened without any delay when we pressed the button. It lifted us back into the sound of travellers and we began following the signs above us to the right terminal. As we drew closer we began to join a movement of people whose clothes indicated they were on their way to the sunshine of Greece. Many were in shorts and sporting sun hats, while the families who looked Greek dressed like people all over the world do who live and work in hot cities. We found ourselves outside a set of sliding doors and to our surprise, realised we had to ride an airport rail shuttle out to the terminal. As it raced through the dark morning we watched technical staff attending to the needs of aircraft which would soon be carrying the likes of us far away.

Outside the shuttle we were faced with a security check, and had to take out any liquids or electronic devices we had on us. After dropping them with our bags into a box which was x-rayed, we were invited to walk through a scanner. As I passed through it the alarm bleeped and a man approached me.

"Empty your pockets please." I began pulling out icon cards, a prayer rope and a wooden cross, and the security man said "Have you got the whole church in there?" I smiled with some relief at his joke, and as he waved his electronic wand over me I was cleared to proceed. I turned to head off only to find Joseph smiling with amusement at my situation.

Once inside the terminal we located our gate and joined the snaking queue that was already fifty or sixty people long. A few glances were thrown my way and I wondered how many of those looking could guess that this bearded priest with a dark complexion was as English they were. Eventually two women in airline uniforms began fussing with their equipment near the exit, and it was clear we were about to be invited forwards. The message board above them changed its message and people began to shuffle slowly ahead to have their passes and passports checked. Beyond their desk was a covered tunnel which was attached to the outside of the aircraft. We were welcomed aboard by two heavily made-up stewardesses and counted down the seat numbers to find our places. A man was sitting there, his briefcase opened out onto the seat beside him. "That's my seat," I announced, to which he said nothing but gathered his possessions and slid over near the window. We stowed our bags away and buckled in, Joseph sitting between me and the man. We quietly watched as the remaining passengers organised themselves, parents fussing over where their children would sit, as the cabin crew pulled shut the swinging door to seal us in. After the usual announcements and safety procedures, we waited just a few minutes before the aeroplane began to reverse away from the terminal. Through the cabin windows we could see how the early morning sun was now lighting up the concrete, and signs of anxiety could be spotted in a few of the faces around us. After a brief pause, we began to roll forwards, quickly picking up speed. The imperfections in the runway surface vibrated through the seats beneath us as the thrust of the engines strained against the demands of gravity. I looked ahead at the stewardesses' faces, searching for any sign of panic, but all was well and we felt the aeroplane's nose lifting from the earth. In seconds we could see the ground falling away beneath us and as we banked a little London filled the windows.

Soon we were flying flat and the sound of the engines subsided. The stewardesses began their rounds of food and drink, and we pretended not to notice how long people were spending in the toilet. The man beside Joseph decided to move to the empty seats behind us which meant we had an uninterrupted view of the clouds. The sharp edges of the alpine mountains passed beneath us, black peaks dressed in cold snow. We saw ships alone on the water, oblivious to anyone spying on them from the skies, and as the hours passed we began to recognise the change in colour of the land that marked our passing from the grey Atlantic to the warm effects of the Aegean Sea. Joseph was deep in thought for much of the flight, and I forced myself not to ask how he was feeling.

Sooner than expected the pilot was announcing that we needed to prepare ourselves for landing, and the stewardesses made their last checks that everything was locked away. The physical sensation of our descent gripped at my stomach, and we could begin to see the roads and buildings of Greece. I leaned over to look past Joseph, and saw the arid hills that seemed to fill so much of the Greek landscape. Once more the aeroplane banked steeply, through the windows on the left the ground was too close, and through the windows on the right there was only sky. We could see Thessalonica airport ahead of us, as we grew closer to the ground. I glanced at Joseph who was staring down ahead of him. As the ground met the wheels we felt a hard jolt that seemed too abrupt for a normal landing, but I was reassured once more with a quick glance into the faces of the stewardesses.

We taxied into position, and two runway buses pulled up alongside us. Everyone found their bags and children, and edged forwards towards the open door. As soon as we stepped out into the open air we were hit with a wall of heat and also the reality of being so far from home. We carefully descended the metal stairs and trotted across to the waiting bus. Inside everyone stood for the one minute ride to the terminal, and looking out across the airport it was obvious how different the cultures of England and Greece are. Back at Gatwick there was an atmosphere of almost military precision, the huge runways and terminals were designed for enormous numbers of travellers. But here in Thessalonica there were shoots of weeds growing up through the runway, rundown buildings could be seen along the fences, and the impression was of a place where appearance wasn't important.

In the welcome shade of the building we queued once more, and at the desk the frowning official began to question me.

"You are English?"

"Yes," I assured him.

His frown grew a little more intense and he began to type something into his computer. He looked again at my passport, then at me, and then back at his screen. There was a horrible pause before he slid the passport back to me and said "Okay." I wondered whether it was an Englishman dressed as an Orthodox priest that bothered him, or perhaps I resembled someone they were looking for. But once I was waved in I quickly headed towards Joseph who was once more watching with an amused expression.

"What was the problem?"

I shook my head, "Don't know, but we're here so let's not worry."

No doubt like at every airport in the world, the road outside was filled with waiting taxis. I leaned into the window of the first one we came to, "Do you speak English?"

The driver, who looked to be in his mid-sixties, pulled a face. "A little," he said. Joseph climbed in the back with the bags and I sat in the front passenger seat. Knowing that there are two bus stations in Thessalonica I explained that we needed the one for Ouranoupolis. It wasn't clear that he completely understood what I was saying, but he nodded and pulled out into the traffic. His dashboard was thick with grime and dust, but stuck in amongst the receipts and wrappers were two icons, one of the Theotokos and one of Saint Paisios.

I pointed to the latter and gladly exclaimed "Saint Paisios!"

The driver nodded, "Yes, he prays for us."

This was enough to relax me, I smiled and happily watched the road ahead of us, taking in as many of the place names as I could. It was only a ten minute journey, and the meter said twelve euros. But before I could find my cash the driver said "Eighteen euros."

I looked at him and hesitated, I felt this devotee of Saint Paisios was suddenly turning into a conman. But having only been in the country for less than half an hour, and not feeling confident with the language, I found the money and thanked him.

The bus station was as run down as I remembered it, on my first trip I had wondered if the taxi driver had left me at the right place. We bought our tickets to Ouranoupolis and went outside to sit in the shade. We had a half hour wait, and it was a good opportunity to stop and take in where we were. A few young men sat not far from us to our left, but further along the benches to our right was a man dressed in black trousers and jumper, with a long straggly beard and grey pony tail. I tried to assess whether he was a monk or a priest, and guessed he was no doubt catching the same bus as us.

Beside the station was a café, and I caught Joseph looking in.

"Are you hungry?" I asked.

"Yea," he nodded, "I'll see what they've got."

"Okay, I'm not, I'll wait here."

He left his bag beside me and disappeared into the shade. I threw another discreet look at the man in black and saw him waving off a middle aged man who was trying to sell him something. I lifted both our bags and strolled towards him, wondering whether he would speak any English.

"Hello, are you waiting for the Ouranoupolis bus?" I asked.

His face opened into a broad smile, "Yes Father, please sit here." His eyes were piercing blue and full of warmth.

As I sat beside him I asked, "Are you visiting Mount Athos?"

He nodded slowly, "Yes, I used to live there."

"Where do you live now?"

He struggled to find the words, "I am in Ukraine. You are English?"

"Yes, we've just arrived."

"From London?" He asked.

"Yes, Gatwick, have you been to London?"

"No, but I would like to. Things are terrible in Ukraine. Since the American CIA put in their people things are very bad. Do you know what is happening?"

I shook my head, "Only a little. The BBC doesn't talk about what's really happening there."

"The new government is fascist, they are murdering Christians." This was the first time I had heard this, I knew there were many accusations about the American-backed government in Ukraine, but persecution of Christians had never come up.

"In the region I come from," (here he named the region and town which I have omitted) "Christians are killed every month. Sometimes three of four bodies in a few weeks, for being Christian."

"I had no idea," I admitted, "why are they doing this? Is it because they see the Orthodox Church being a sign of Russian influence?"

"Maybe they do, but that is not why they kill us. It is not only Orthodox, all Christians are targeted. Even Jehovah's Witnesses have been killed. Anyone they think is Christian, even if they are not. This is why I am returning to the Holy Mountain, if I stayed in my town any longer I knew I would be killed. I abandoned my church there, I am a priest, if I ever go back they will kill me. Do you understand? For being a priest they will take my life."

Had I not heard it from his own mouth I would have found it difficult to believe. The mainstream media was saying nothing, in fact the new Ukrainian government was painted as an ally in the unending anti-Russian rhetoric. Again I shook my head, and could say nothing but "This is terrible."

Despite what he was saying, he smiled gently, his eyes full of intelligence and perception. "I am going to ask advice from my spiritual father, I must find a new place to live. Do you think England is a Christian country?"

"Not any more. They have taught the people to try and live without God."

"Yes," he nodded, "this is happening all across Europe. The United Nations has a big plan for us all. But they do not understand that God's plan is bigger." He chuckled to himself. "We are living in dangerous times, and the majority of people have closed their eyes to what is happening. Very dangerous."

As he was speaking Joseph appeared with a pastry, without any hesitation he introduced himself. "Hello Father, I'm Father's son."

The Ukranian priest got to his feet and gave him a blessing. "What is your name?"

"Joseph, and yours?"

"I am Father I., and yours Father?"

I stood and introduced myself, and we took our seats again. Joseph was keen to engage with him. "Are you from Mount Athos?"

"Yes, I have lived there for eight years. You have been before?"

"No, this is my first visit, my dad's been though."

As Joseph was speaking our bus pulled up, throwing a cloud of dust towards us from the dry yard. Without further conversation Father I. walked quickly to the open door of the bus and handed his ticket to the driver. A second man was helping passengers push their bags into the storage area in the side of the bus, and rather nervously I handed him my bag containing my money, passports, and everything else that seemed vital. The tickets were for specific seats, and though it was barely half full, everyone seemed intent on finding the right number. As we eased into ours, we watched as two monks emerged from the bus station and climbed aboard. One of them took a seat a few rows in front of us and I took the opportunity to study him. He looked to be in his seventies, but it was hard to tell as his thin body and sunken face looked warn out beyond his years. Even before the bus pulled away he leaned his head against the window and began to sleep. I imagined how few hours he had been in his bed during the night, and understood that here was a small sign of that other life they were leading.

Around the edges of the driver's window were stuck many icons, and from his rear view mirror hung a prayer rope and a crucifix. In England such displays of faith would be considered odd or extreme, but in Orthodox Greece it was ordinary.

It was another fifteen minutes before the bus finally pulled away, and I felt the sense of movement towards Athos once more. One of the final passengers to board was an overweight man in his forties who took the seat directly across the aisle from us. Within a few minutes of the bus moving he turned to me and in a strong Australian accent said "Father, do you speak English?"

The question made me smile, "Yes, I'm English."

He looked surprised, "English Orthodox! You are heading to Mount Athos I presume?"

"Yes, we're catching the ferry tomorrow."

"That's what I was hoping to ask you about Father, which port are you leaving from?"

"Ouranoupolis," I told him, "what about you?"

"I'm entering from the other side of the peninsula, but I'm not sure which stop to get off at."

"I'm sorry, I don't know." I turned to locate Father I., and indicating who I meant said "That priest speaks good English, he should be able to help you."

He thanked me and went to ask what he needed. A few minutes later he returned, "Thanks Father, all sorted."

"Good," I smiled.

"Do you mind me asking Father, where abouts in England are you from?"

"Herefordshire, near the Midlands."

"Oh right, I've spent time in London, but never ventured that far north. What's your parish like up there?"

"It's small. Made up of a mixture of Greeks, Russians, Romanians, Bulgarians and English converts. We worship in English, as that's the one language we all share."

He slid over to the seat nearer to the aisle, "Are you a convert?"

"Yes, from Anglicanism, about fifteen years ago. What about you?"

"No," he shook his head, "I'm not anything. I'm visiting Athos because I'm studying monastic life. I've just spent two months in Tibet, at the moment I'd call myself a Buddhist if I'm anything."

I began to wonder how he would react to the life of the monks so filled with Christ's presence. "Have you been to Mount Athos before?"

"No, I wrote to one of the monasteries and told them about my studies. They were very open to my enquiries, but I don't know what to expect. I'm interested in comparing the practice of the Jesus Prayer with Buddhist meditation."

As he said this I was relieved the monk ahead of us was sleeping, it seemed such an inappropriate statement. "Orthodoxy sees the two very differently," I said.

"I'm sure they do," he acknowledged, "but from an objective perspective there are many similarities."

"I don't know how it's possible to understand the Jesus Prayer in an objective way. It is a very personal, subjective experience. We believe it is about relationship with God, whereas Buddhism has as its goal the disciplining of the self."

"Yea sure," he said, "but they're both about discipline and self-control. That's the connection I'm interested in."

"The monks you visited in Tibet, did they believe in God?"

"No, they see the responsibility for change as being theirs alone."

"I'm sure you'll bring this up with the fathers on Athos, they'll be able to explain the difference better than me." I hesitated, knowing I couldn't answer his points entirely. "But saying the Jesus Prayer isn't about emptying ourselves, it is a way of focussing on God's presence, reminding ourselves Who it is we are living before. I don't think it will be possible to really understand the Jesus Prayer before grasping what it means to Orthodox people to live in the presence of God."

He wasn't hearing the kinds of responses he hoped for and I sensed he was losing interest in the conversation. "I hope you find everything you need," I added. I sensed Joseph beside me wanting to say something but holding himself back. There was really no need for us to say anything, the coming days would reveal to him all that was necessary. I hoped the journey would bring him more answers than he anticipated.

The bus route took us through typical Greek villages, their white walls and terracotta rooves looking like every Greek picture postcard. On top of most of the homes were perched large metal water barrels with solar panels above them. As beautiful as the houses looked, it was impossible not to notice the level of graffiti which defaced so many walls. Even in UK inner cities it is rare to see this amount of writing scrawled so close to where people live, and I wondered how much of the Greek lettering was youth related, and how much expressed the anger felt at the Greek economic situation. Eventually we saw the first sign for Ouranoupolis and then as we emerged from behind an arid hill the Aegean Sea came into view.

The Australian got to his feet and wished us a safe journey. The bus pulled over to the side of the road and we watched him retrieving his bag from the side of the bus. There wasn't much indication of a hotel, and his face revealed his concern about where he should go. But before he could make up his mind the driver had quickly returned and had us back out on the road.

Before I had seen it for myself, I had heard unimpressive descriptions of Ouranoupolis, and it wasn't until I visited that I found they were unfounded. As we reached the outskirts we saw many hotels built along the road, all of which looked clean and in good repair. The town's main square sits beneath an old tower that has become the symbol for the town. The bus pulled round in front of a few parked cars, and I glanced around at the shops and sea front, happy to recognise much of it.

Once we had grabbed our bags I pointed a few places out to Joseph. "That's the road for the pilgrim's office, we have to pick up our entrance certificates tomorrow." I turned back and pointed down what looked like a side street, "The port's down there, where we catch the ferry."

Joseph followed me along the path above the beech, I had booked us into the same hotel I had previously stayed at, and I was keen to see it again as the memories from my first visit came flooding back. Up a small street that ran at a right angle to the main road I spotted the balcony where I had enjoyed my breakfast three years before. The reception area was air conditioned, and we were happy to wait behind a group of four Russian priests who were signing in. The walls around us were filled with expensive looking icons and photographs of monks. The young woman taking their details spoke fluent Russian, and as they signed their names they glanced our way and bowed in acknowledgement to us. The receptionist's English was as good as her Russian, and I handed her my passport which she said they needed for ten minutes so that they could make a copy. I couldn't remember this happening before, and I was a little uneasy handing it over, but the relief from having arrived safely overcame my anxiety. While we waited for her to return, Father I. the Ukrainian priest entered, his face erupting into a huge smile of recognition, as though we had known each other for years rather than met earlier at a bus station.

"I have no reservation," he began to tell us, "do you think they will have room?"

"I don't know Father, we've only just arrived ourselves."

The woman returned and handed me my passport. As I was putting it away I listened to her telling Father I. that there were no rooms available. The disappointment in his voice was clear, but he turned to us once more and said "We must meet later for coffee."

"That would be nice," I said, and a little uncomfortably we turned and abandoned him to his fate as we headed to our room. On the walls of the corridors were hung large paintings of Athonite monasteries, and it was clear that the hotel was a stop-off point for pilgrims. Our room was simple but clean, and in my usual fashion I headed straight to the shower to check its condition. Meanwhile Joseph had pulled back the curtains and stepped out onto the balcony.

"Dad," he shouted, "come and look at this."

I followed him out and found we were looking directly over the local church. Its light red tiles topped a beautiful white building with a similar coloured square tower. Around the windows was painted a dark purple frame, and out in front fluttered the Byzantine and Greek flags. Beyond the church were the low roofs of houses and hotels, and beyond them shimmered the sea. We looked to our left, and peeping out of a light mist was the peak of Athos, looking like it was floating above the water.

Chapter 3

We decided to take a walk around the town, I wanted to be sure I had remembered the location of the pilgrim's office correctly, but also that it hadn't been moved. As we emerged from the stairs into the reception area the young woman asked if we would want breakfast in the morning. We talked it over and decided we would rather find something elsewhere. The evening was still light but a cool breeze was now bringing the temperature down to what Englishman find comfortable. We followed the side road down to the sea front and began walking back to where the bus had dropped us off. Our gaze was fixed on the small fishing boats resting on the sand, and we failed to spot Father I. sitting at a café across the road from us.

"Hello Father Spyridon," he shouted, "come for a drink."

We turned to the sound of his voice and waved in response. Crossing the road I asked "Did you find a room?"

"Yes, yes, no problem. Will you join me?"

"We're just heading up to the pilgrim's office, how long will you be here?"

"It's shut now," he told us, "come and sit down."

"I know, we just want to be sure we can find it in the morning."

"Ah yes," he nodded, "I will wait for you."

We quickened our pace past the bars and now closed gift shops, making a mental note of the many windows filled with icons.

"Can we do some shopping when we come back from Athos?" Joseph asked.

"Definitely, but we won't be able to buy anything bigger than we can take on the 'plane."

The pilgrim's office was still on the corner where it had been on my last visit, and it felt good to confirm that the hotel was only a five minute walk away. Instead of going directly back to Father I. we followed the path round the office, down to the little window where tickets for the ferry are sold. Again, it felt good knowing where everything was, I was dealing with that irrational fear that something might go wrong when planning something important. We walked on down past the concrete peer where a few boats were tied up for the night. I enjoyed being able to point out to Joseph from where the ferry would depart, as a parent I wanted him to feel secure in the knowledge that everything was in hand. We went on past the old tower, and there ahead of us sat Father I. enjoying his coffee.

"Hello again Father," I said as we walked up behind him, "would you like another drink?"

"No, thank you, too much caffeine at this hour will keep me awake."

As we sat Joseph asked "What was it like living on Athos?"

"Happy, very happy." It was obvious he wanted to express it differently, but his grasp of English wouldn't allow anything more accurate. "The monks live like angels there. Angels on earth. Of course there are problems at times, because we are still men, but nowhere else have I found such harmony."

Joseph smiled as he listened.

A young waitress came out to take our orders, and we both asked for coffee. Father I. continued, "It is the duty of every Christian to seek God. Not just pray a little, or think about God now and then. We are created to know God, to love God, this is a requirement of us. We who are Christian must make this the most important priority in our lives. If we allow ourselves to become distracted by the world we can lose sight of our true purpose." He glanced at us both to make sure we were following his words. I nodded encouragement. "This is the life on Athos, everything is provided for men to meet with God. When I was asked to leave to care for the parish in Ukraine, my heart was broken for a while, I did not want to leave. But of course, we must do as we're told. I served the people there for as long as I could, but now I am returning to ask to be released from this obedience. If I return to Ukraine I will be killed, and I do not yet feel ready to die."

The waitress appeared with a tray and laid out our cups in front of us along with glasses of water. The coffee was thick and sweet, and we took a few sips as Father I. spoke.

"There is a corruption in world politics which goes unnoticed." His face became more serious as he spoke. "The people of Ukraine have experienced all this before when Lenin sent his Jewish thugs to persecute the Church. They tortured the bishops and killed as many Christians as they could find. This is not a new thing that we are seeing now. But who knows, the history books may once more be filled with blank pages when it comes to the treatment of the Church. I do not think this world has long to go, but then my grandparents thought the same thing under the communists. How much more suffering God will ask of us we cannot know, but for now we must pray and hold on to our faith. People in the West do not understand what is happening because it has been hidden from them for many years. But their time will come, and may God preserve them when it does."

Aware of our reaction he smiled once more, and sipped at his water. "Which monasteries are you staying at?"

"We're going to St. Panteleimon first, and then..." Before I could finish he grinned and cut in.

"It is God's will, I am visiting Panteleimon tomorrow. Have you been there before?"

"No, this is our first time."

"I know the monks there very well, you will like this monastery. The icons are very holy, many miracles have occurred through the prayers of the Mother of God. Of course, it is the Russian monastery, so you know the choir will be good." He laughed at himself, but there was an obvious pride in what he was saying. I was struck by how quickly his mood had lightened after telling us about what he had experienced, there was no hint of moroseness or sentimentality. As he reached for his remaining coffee I noticed the long black prayer rope that he was holding beneath the table, and I knew that even as he sat talking to us he was praying.

"Father," Joseph asked, "can you say something about prayer?"

Father I. paused for a moment as he gathered his thoughts. "I am no master, but I can say a little. First, when we seek to pray, we must always do so with love. And if we have no love, we must try to love. Prayer without love for God and our neighbour is empty. It is love that God wants from us, and only with a loving heart do we really draw close to God in prayer."

"Do you mean that God doesn't listen to us if we don't have love Father?" Joseph asked.

"No, of course God hears everything, even the movements of our hearts that we do not notice. But we are not open to God if we do not love. Too many times we pray with nothing but concern for ourselves. In fact, too often our whole spiritual life is really just about satisfying ourselves. We seek salvation because we are full of ego, it is really just a desire for our own wellbeing. We must move beyond this, so that everything we do is for God's glory. We must even dare to seek our own salvation for God alone. Every saint is illuminated by God, they shine with His light and to His glory. Our hearts are the one place in the whole universe where God's glory can only shine if we permit it.

So we must pray, repent, fast, do all of the things that the Church teaches us, so that God is glorified in one more place, here in our hearts." He gently patted his chest to emphasise his point. He continued, "Too often the world makes us afraid, and when we are frightened we begin to think of our worldly needs, we begin to act like no more than animals. This is why we must guard ourselves against fear. Remember how the angels again and again said "Do not fear!" To the shepherds, and to the Theotokos herself. We must drive away fear so that we are not ruled by the demands of this world. And only when we overcome fear can we truly love, and only when we love can we pray. Do you understand?"

Joseph nodded, "Yes Father, but must we become monks to pray like this? How can we do it in the world?"

"There are many saints who have lived in the world, God can make saints in any situation. But the distractions of the world are difficult to combat, especially in our modern world." Joseph and I nodded our agreement. He continued, "It isn't just the things of the world, the demands of family life, dealing with jobs and money, these things can be good if they are used to serve God. But we can detect a way of thinking that is becoming dominant in the West that is hostile to authentic Christianity." He looked into the distance for a moment, collecting his thoughts. "People are being trained to constantly seek comfort and entertainment, the satisfaction of their own desires is becoming the goal of human life. The Enlightenment placed man at the centre of the universe, and now man's desires have become supreme. Being raised with this outlook makes it very hard for children to grow up and be willing to embrace the demands of Christianity. Self-renunciation is not just for monks, but all of us. Christ called us to take up our cross, which means crucifying our pride, our lust and selfishness. This is what the saints teach us, we only have to look at their lives and see all of this. Many of them followed Christ even to death, they considered their physical life as nothing compared with union with God. We in the West are a pale imitation of the generations of Christians who went before us. Our faith is weak and we run frightened when Christ asks us too much of us. But still there are martyrs, even today. You see? Even in this modern world that is so distorted, God gives us saints and martyrs. So we must not lose hope, for God all things are possible." He smiled and pointed at himself, "What miracles God can do even with men like us."

His smile was contagious, we could feel our hearts being lifted by his words. "Thank you Father," Joseph said, "that is helpful."

"Don't think I have much wisdom to share," Father I.'s face became serious, "I am only repeating what I am taught by others. We can learn these words, but allowing them to move from our lips to our hearts is quite another thing. On the Holy Mountain there are monks who have been made truly wise, because wisdom comes only when we know God. Our thoughts do not contain wisdom, the mind must be illuminated by Christ. I pray you will meet those who are truly wise; you will know the difference between simple monks like me and hearts that are filled with Christ's presence."

The coffees were finished and Father I. got to his feet, "I hope we can meet tomorrow, I would like to speak some more."

"Thank you," I said, "we would appreciate that."

"When we give ourselves to the mystery of God, we begin to see things in a new way, and God slowly gives us a new way of seeing. But we mustn't try to rush things, the mysteries of God cannot be snatched at, we must be patient." He looked at his bill and placed some coins on top of it. Joseph extended his hands to receive a blessing and then kissed Father I.'s hand. Without another word Father I. turned and walked towards his hotel. I glanced at our bill and fished out the right change from my pocket. The evening sky was beginning to darken and we crossed the road to look out at the peak of Athos one more time.

"Are you hungry?" I asked.

"Yea, I could do with something."

We found a small supermarket and bought some bread rolls and sliced ham along with four cans of Mythos beer. We were aware of how quiet the town was as we strolled past the empty restaurants. One of the waiters called out to us as we passed, desperate for custom. I held the shopping bag aloft and smiled, to which he gave a wave of resignation.

Instead of walking straight back to the hotel we swung round so that we could see if the church was unlocked. We climbed the steps and as I pushed the large wooden door it slowly opened. Inside we could hear a lone voice chanting in Greek. We peered into the gloom and could make out a single candle burning behind the iconostasis, but the shadows were too deep to make out much else. We quietly let ourselves in but no sooner had we entered than the voice went silent and the candle was blown out. I feared we had interrupted someone's prayers but when the priest emerged through the Deacon's Door he was unaware of our presence. He looked to be in his late sixties with a very long white beard. He slowly bowed and kissed the icon of Christ, and as he turned to leave I announced our presence.

"Good evening Father."

He was a little startled but then began speaking in very quick Greek as he continued to head for the door. Once there he stopped and pulled out a large key which he inserted in the outside of the lock. We quickly followed him out and watched him lock up. He said something more in Greek, turned and was gone. Joseph and I looked at each other and smiled.

Back in our hotel room I found a knife and cut open the rolls. Without butter the bread was dry, but the beer helped it go down. We sat out on the balcony watching the sky darken further over the sea, happy to take in the scene without too many words. Across the church roof from us the large black cross on top of the church bell tower was now silhouetted against the moonlight reflected on the shimmering water. It had been a long day and we were both ready for bed. I set the alarm clock for 7am and with a cool breeze coming through the open balcony window, we quickly got to sleep.

Chapter 4

We woke refreshed and ready. I had woken a few minutes before the alarm and turned it off before it could sound the start of the day. It gave me time to think about where we were going and a tremendous sense of excitement passed over me. I stepped out onto the balcony to discover low clouds had filled the sky and a steady drizzle was falling. We were washed and packed in twenty minutes and for a second time in two days we went to reception to hand in our key. The Russian priests were seated at a table with vast amounts of food in front of them, no doubt stocking up for the Athonite diet ahead. Once outside we kept our heads down as the rain was now falling harder, the first poor weather I had experienced in a Greek summer.

We retraced our route from the evening before and with great relief found the pilgrim's office both open and free of customers. The interior was divided in two by a single long counter behind which the three officials sat staring into their computer monitors. As we approached the nearest man said something in Greek and pointed to the other end of the counter. Before reaching the official now looking up at us we retrieved our passports. In order to enter Mount Athos pilgrims must have a certificate called a diamonitirion, a beautifully embossed document without which it is not possible to even board the ferry. Only one hundred Orthodox men are issued with these each day (though that number does not include clerics) and also ten non-Orthodox.

The next official looked back at his monitor as he spoke, "Passport!"

I slid it over and he quickly checked the details. He handed it back to me and nodded before glancing at Joseph and once more repeating his request which he would have to say at least a hundred and nine more times that morning. As he handed Joseph's back to him he pointed to the other end of the counter. We followed the direction of his gesture and the man at that end asked for our names. He clicked away at his keyboard and suddenly stopped. "Are you a student?" He asked Joseph. Sensing there was a problem I butted in, "He's twenty-two, he's my son."

The official gave me a cursory glance and repeated his question. "Are you a student?"

"Yes, I am." As Joseph gave his answer I began wondering what would be the right thing to do if only one of us was given the chance to enter the Holy Mountain. Before another word was spoken I was estimating how much money I had on me and whether I could afford to put Joseph up in a hotel for three days. But I didn't need to reveal my terrible thoughts, the official broke out into a grin, he was enjoying the obvious panic in our faces, "Students may receive a discount in price. Do you have your student card?"

Even as Joseph said he didn't have it on him the relief we experienced more than made up for the few euros we could have saved. The printer whirred and clicked beside him and he handed us our certificates. We thanked him and stashed them away in my bag. The rain was still falling heavily and so we decided to eat breakfast near the ferry ticket office where we could sit beneath the large awnings. The scene we approached was busy and male. It looked like every passenger who was catching the ferry had had the same impulse. Groups of men, a tenth of whom were either priests or monks, were noisily eating or ordering breakfast as the two or three waitresses rushed back and forth. We found an empty table and immediately became aware of the different languages being used around us. It was Friday, and we scanned the menu to find the non-meat dishes. We didn't recognise many of the names and when the young waitress came to serve us we had her run through the options and identify which foods were meat and dairy free. They were clearly used to Orthodox customers as they had a good variety available, and when she assured us that certain dishes were permitted on fast days I happily took her word for it (though I had my doubts).

As we were eating the ticket office opened and we watched a disorderly crowd gather around the little window. There was a little ill-tempered pushing at one point but nothing came of it. By the time we had eaten the crowd had thinned down and I went over to collect the tickets I had booked. The woman selling the tickets traced a column of names with her finger and found our names and numbers. She tore off the tickets from a roll and we had everything we needed. I returned to Joseph and we ordered a leisurely second drink. From our seats we could see the pier and until the ferry arrived we knew there was no rush. Departure time was 10am and at around twenty minutes before this groups started leaving their tables to queue. Knowing that seating was limited on the ferry I suggested we risk the light rain that was falling so that we might have some cover out on the sea. By the time we got there the ferry was pulling in, the same one I had ridden three years before. The front gate lowered and a few Greek deck-hands began giving loud instructions to some van drivers who were to be permitted to board first. Although the monks of Athos grow their own food, even they rely on certain provisions and resources being brought from the mainland.

The shuffling queue soon brought Joseph and me to the deck-hand asking to see everyone's certificates and passports. The realisation that Athos is a separate state unto itself is reinforced with such formalities, and once there pilgrims enter a time zone based on Byzantine time, where the new day begins at vespers each evening. He quickly checked our documents and tickets and waved us through. The ideal location on the ferry in sunny weather is the top deck beneath the sun shade, but with rain still falling everyone was squeezing into the restaurant. Seating was limited but we managed to find a spot where we could see through the open doorway to watch Athos coming closer.

The ferry was late leaving, and so many wet men cramped into a room not designed for such a number quickly turned the air stale. But such things were quickly forgotten when the rumble of the engines fired up and we felt ourselves reversing away from the pier. Joseph wandered off to buy a coffee, and I watched with a sense of relief, here was one of my sons on his way to the Holy Mountain. For the first half hour there was little conversation amongst the pilgrims, the windows were clouded with condensation and only the occasional brave soul ventured out to take in the view. But as we got closer to our destination the rain became intermittent and it seemed worth braving.

"Joe, do you want to go up on the deck?"

"Definitely," he said already getting to his feet. We climbed the metal steps up to the top of the ferry and found the rain was barely noticeable in the warm air. We found a spot besides the railing and watched as the peninsula passed before us. By the time the first of the monasteries came into view the rain had cleared and a number of men were coming out to enjoy the sights. The first few monasteries looked like they were built directly next to the beach, their small size and irregular shapes made them appear welcoming and very human. Of course, the quaint perspective I was seeing them with had nothing to do with the spiritual warfare that was being conducted within. These gentle looking buildings concealed the harsh struggles of lifestyles that would terrify many of us.

Now that the pilgrims had moved outside two monks set up their stalls. They unrolled blankets at each end of the deck and began selling prayer ropes and crosses. Joseph went over and began looking through what was on sale. On the hill was a small hut with a well-kept garden beneath it, and I began to think of the hermits struggling in solitude. When I looked back at Joseph he was in deep conversation with one of the monks, who was explaining something in detail to him. When he returned I asked him if everything was okay and he simply said "Yea, great."

Rising out of the clouds and mist the peak of the Holy Mountain was now looming over us in all its glory. Despite it being May there were still streaks of snow running down its gullies, and near the summit could be seen a small building. Three well-built priests began hovering near us trying to decide on the best angle for a group photograph with the mountain behind them. They began taking it in turns taking shots of one another, and so I offered to take one of them together. In Russian they expressed their gratitude, and as I clicked the shutter I imagined them showing the photograph to their friends back home. With any embarrassment about posing for photographs now removed, Joseph and I followed suit and captured our moment in such a beautiful scene.

On its way to the port of Daphne, where most pilgrims enter Athos, the ferry calls in at the monasteries along the coast. As we felt the bow turning into shore we watched a monk in a small inflatable motor boat bobbing over the waves at some speed. A few on board pulled out their cameras to capture the moment. The ferry slowly pulled up to the short wooden pier and four pilgrims climbed ashore to disappear into the monastery. The whole process took less than a minute and we were once more reversing out to sea.

As we sailed I was counting off the monasteries and checking on my small map of Athos so that we didn't miss the Monastery of Saint Panteleimon; but when it came into view I knew I needn't have worried. Anyone who has looked at a photograph of this huge Russian monastery can be in no doubt when they see it. Even from a distance it looks almost too large to be crouching as it does next to the beach. Its green rooves and onion domes top three and four storey buildings that look more permanent and solid than the yellow stoned walls of the other monasteries on this part of the peninsula. The small windows in the walls are so numerous and regular that there is almost an impression of military exactness, and as the ferry approached this impression only grew.

We lifted our bags to our shoulders and carefully descended the wet, slippery stairways. On the lowest deck we eased passed the other pilgrims who were staying on until Daphne, and made our way to the front of the ferry as it drew up to the concrete pier jutting out into the sea. From this lower viewpoint the monastery now seemed to tower overhead as we looked up at it, and then the full view of pier came into view as the heavy metal gate lowered before us. In all about twenty pilgrims alighted, and once more the captain of the ferry wasted no time in pulling up the gate and reversing away. As we began to climb the slight incline to the monastery a huge bulldozer headed towards us. The group scattered to each side of the road and as it passed we could see the driver was a heavily bearded young monk wearing black wraparound sunglasses. He trundled by and to our left we could see some kind of construction work underway.

At the top of the first pathway we were faced with a T junction and the group came to a stop as pairs and groups began trying to decide which way to go. But from behind us emerged Father I. who took the pathway to the right announcing "This way." Everyone followed behind him and as we reached a large arched entrance I turned back to see the ferry disappearing as it followed the shoreline out of view. Closer to the monastery the sound of construction machinery became quite loud, but as soon as we entered the shade of one of the buildings the noise was blocked out. There were no signs indicating which direction we should take but the confidence of Father I. was enough to assure the whole group we were being led the right way.

The trail took us to a flat grassed area through the middle of which was a narrow pathway along both sides of which grew an abundance of colourful flowers. Everything looked pristine, the result of many hours of care and attention. This has been my experience in all the monasteries I have visited on Athos, the environment is treated as something which impacts us deeply, and so an attempt is made to maintain a sense of beauty, in stone, paintings and gardens. To the right of the pathway was a single-story drop to the bottom of one of the buildings across which iron foot bridges gave access to a walkway that ran along the outside of the structure. We all crossed one of the bridges to enter through a large doorway at the side of which was a sign in Russian, Greek and English which read "There is no blessing for photographs to be taken in the monastery grounds. This is to be strictly observed."

Inside we walked through a large foyer from which steps went to the upper and lower floors. The interior was decorated with a sombre, dark wood, and immediately even the polite chatter of the group came to an end. A young monk beckoned for us to go through another doorway, which led to a small refectory where coffee, biscuits and jars of cold water were placed on the tables. In the middle of the room there was also a tray of small spirit glasses containing the same powerful liquid I had tasted on the peninsula before. To my surprise the majority of men went straight for the coffee, and I felt a little self-conscious knocking back a glass of the fire water.

Joseph was now sitting opposite Father I. and as I approached I found they were deep in conversation. Groups were forming a queue to check in at a counter behind which the young monk was standing next to a grey bearded old monk who was checking pilgrims' passports and assigning them rooms. The process was being completed very slowly, and like a few others, I decided to sit and wait. Father I. was now dressed in his rassa, and looked like he had never left the Holy Mountain. He broke off from his conversation and gave me his usual welcoming smile.

"You must drink some coffee," he instructed me, "it is good for you." He laughed to himself and reached over to a pot from which he poured my drink. "I have not let them know I was coming, so I do not know if they will have a room for me. If not I will have to walk to another monastery. But I do not think there will be a problem, even with so many pilgrims. They told me they have many staying at the moment."

After seeing him leave the hotel without securing a room, I felt concerned for him, but could see that he had no anxiety about it. It was something of a lesson for me, as I have a tendency to want everything planned carefully enough to avoid all unwanted surprises: little did I know how our pilgrimage was to unfold. A monk once instructed me that often our flaws or passions are the flip side of our virtues. So someone who is very organised and reliable may be tempted to be too controlling. Or someone who is very sensitive to the feelings of other people may fall into the sin of man-pleasing. It is a useful way to examine ourselves, by recognising our strengths we can also reflect on our weaknesses or the weaknesses we may be vulnerable to. Seeing Father I. able to live with what would feel like too much uncertainty to me made me recognise that trust in God requires us to sometimes give up what we hold on to for security. Security can only truly be found in Him. After Father I.'s experiences in Ukraine, the small matter of where he was going to sleep tonight was hardly worth losing peace over – but I knew if it was me, I still would.

Joseph lifted the bowl of biscuits and offered me one before doing the same to Father I. who shook his head and looked at me. "You see that Father, your son has manners. England must be a good place to live with such manners. We had a group of American students staying with us who had no manners at all." He demonstrated what he meant by pretending to grab at the biscuits and wildly force them into his mouth.

I laughed at his antics and said "They're not all like that Father, I've met some lovely Americans. And the truth is not all young people in England are any better than that."

He pursed his lips, "Maybe, but it is good to see manners."

Joseph was looking down into his coffee cup, embarrassed by the comments, but clearly amused by what was happening.

Father I. became serious once more, already we were learning to sense the change in his expression and tone of voice that indicated when his words were revealing something that was important to him. "Poor manners can be a sign of a lack of inner attentiveness. When we act without control, even in apparently small things, we are not truly aware of our actions. Our outer life must be ordered, how else can we hope to have spiritual order? We must love God, but this must be joined to attention to all our thoughts and impulses. There must be harmony between what we do and our hearts. This can only be achieved when we are watchful over both. So, when we find ourselves being lazy, or impulsive, we must examine the inner movement of our heart and question ourselves like a ruthless attorney." He smiled at the image, "Only when we see the truth of ourselves do we make progress towards God. This is why I become frustrated sometimes when I hear confession. People just come with long lists, but it is not enough. We must open ourselves to the examination of God, pull aside our defences and look with honesty at who we are."

I was becoming aware of the queue at the window thinning out, but I knew if I turned to look it would bring to an end what Father I. was saying. I ignored the impulse to check, and nodded encouragement, hoping he would say more.

"The Fathers teach us that the body must become the slave of the soul," he continued. "Even when a monk sleeps his heart can be attentive to the prayer within him. I speak here from the Fathers, I do not claim to have reached such heights. We hear people talking about spiritual warfare, but the battle begins here in the guarding of our heart. The demons wish to confuse us, they want to lead us astray. They do not want us to find God, and so they lay traps for us. If we do not guard our mind and heart we can fall into many traps." Unexpectedly he laughed once more and said "We must guard our lips too, but can there be a monk who speaks as much as me?"

"We are grateful for all that you have said Father," I said, "thank you for sharing with us."

"No, it is not me you must thank, these are not my teachings. As I told you, I am only repeating what others have taught me, I am truly a beginner in all things."

There was no false humility about his statement, it was very obvious he believed what he was saying. And in his humility the power of his words only struck us more deeply.

Father I. gestured to the window, "You must get your key. I will wait here until everyone is finished and see if they have room for me."

We smiled and thanked him once more, and leaving our bags at the table joined the two remaining pilgrims at the window. There was still a small group of Russian men at one table, apparently oblivious to the size of the queue, drinking coffee and talking in deep voices about something very serious. We eventually stepped up to the window and the old monk addressed me in Greek.

"I only speak English," I said, offering him our passports. He nodded as the young monk spoke quietly in his ear in Russian, and without any fuss handed us a large key with a plastic fob marked with the number of our room. I thanked them and turned back to our table to find that Father I. was gone. We collected our things as the Russians began to casually saunter over to the window. We went back out to the stairways and tried to identify which floor our room was on. But the numbering wasn't clear, and in the end we had to guess. We descended the stone stairway and found ourselves looking down long corridors in both directions. To our right was a stone sink with a large brass tap. Our room was the second one along and it was left unlocked. One of the privileges afforded to Orthodox clergy is a room to themselves, and so Joseph and I didn't have to share with two or three others. In some situations having to share can be a good way of meeting people, but I was grateful for a private space in which we could relax and talk informally. The room had a high ceiling, painted white like the walls, with a single icon of the Theotokos hanging over one of the wooden beds. The single window reached from the height of the bed almost to the ceiling, and through it we could see down onto the Aegean Sea. The room was comfortably shaded, which only intensified the glow of light that seemed to fill the air outside. There was also a desk, chair and wardrobe, the same items of furniture I have seen in all of the rooms I have stayed in on Athos.

We kicked off our boots and I took off my rassa. Although it was still early, it felt good to lie down and catch my breath. Joseph sat on his bed and asked "What time does the next service start?"

"I don't know, there was a notice on the wall at the bottom of the stairs. Why don't you take a look?"

"Do you mean by the sink?" When I nodded he left to check it out. It was the first chance I had had to be alone, and I tried to become aware of the silence around me. I was aware that in this building and all of the others here, there were men praying, and I wanted nothing more than to cast off the unwanted thoughts and concerns I had carried with me from the world. I threw my feet over the edge of the bed and sat up to pray. The beauty of the peninsula, the impressions of the monasteries, all of it was secondary to the desire to be with God. At last, now that we had stopped moving, I was able to turn to Him.

Chapter 5

Joseph let himself back into the room as quietly as he could, pushing the door slowly back so as to disturb no one down the hall. Once the room was sealed he said "There's a service to venerate the relics in half an hour."

"Does it say where we're meant to go?"

"No, but there'll be plenty of people heading that way. We can tag along."

I pulled my rassa back on and found my hat, "Shall we have a wander up?"

We climbed the stairway back to the floor above us and crossed the narrow bridge towards the other buildings. As we approached them we sensed the full size of the monastery which seemed more like a small town than a single institution. The path took us up to an archway in a high wall, and either side of the entrance were huge icons. We venerated them before entering and found ourselves in a dark walkway that led to another arch on the other side. To our left was a small window at which sat a monk who paid us no attention, and to our right we were surprised to find a shop.

"Shall we have a quick look in?" I asked. Joseph nodded and we entered a small room filled with prayer ropes, crosses, and small icons. A young monk stood behind a counter and a till, and to our left was a doorway through which we could see much larger icons. The monk handed a pilgrim a carrier bag decorated with the name of the monastery, and I made a mental note to obtain one of these for a deacon back home called Panteleimon. As time was short we decided to return another time and resumed our search for the location of the first service.

Outside and through the second arch was an area enclosed by two large buildings, one of which was a church with an impressive bell tower. We assumed that this would be where the service was to be held, but noticed pilgrims gathering at some steps ahead of us. As we joined them we saw a young monk, barely old enough to grow a beard, waiting in the middle of the group. On his belt hung a walkie-talkie, which I imagined was there to call for help in case any of the visitors started causing trouble. After a few minutes he began to address the gathered group, but since he spoke Russian we had no idea what he was saying. He pointed to various things around us, and the Russian pilgrims looked with interest, but then a priest approached me and began speaking to me in broken Greek which was barely better than my own.

"Do you speak English?" I found myself asking once more.

"Yes, Father," his accent was French.

"Do you know what he is saying?"

"Only in my heart," he smiled.

The young monk led the group up the steps towards a small building, and once there he stopped and began what looked even in Russian like a practiced speech. He unlocked the door with a large key hanging from his belt, and reverently the pilgrims entered one by one. I followed Joseph in and found myself surrounded by shelves of skulls. Each wall was filled, and even without a grasp of Russian it was obvious that this was where the young monk's bones would one day end up along with all the others.

The monk was silent as we entered, and we were each left to contemplate the reality of our mortality as we looked into the stripped, fleshless faces of the monks who had once lived and prayed here. In a hushed voice the monk led us to the far end of the room where a series of boxes were opened to reveal holy relics. The skull of Saint Panteleimon stood out amongst them, and the group queued to venerate each of them in turn. I took out the prayer rope I had carried on my last visit to Athos, and after bowing and kissing the holy objects, I gently rubbed it across the relics to bless it. The French priest beside me was doing the same, and said "We have the same idea." Knowing that these saints are now living before God, I brought to mind the reality of their closeness, and even those whose names I didn't know, I believed were holding us before God in their prayers. To be so close to the physical remains of people who now stand with Christ brings heaven into the room, the possibility of salvation is brought near. The solemn atmosphere was extraordinary, every sound and movement felt imbued with reverence, and it became almost impossible not to pray.

We stepped back out into the sunshine, where the pilgrims were quietly sitting around, waiting for the monk to see everyone out. He glanced up at us and then led us down the steps and across towards the church. But instead of going in he stopped and pointed up at the tower which he was now talking about. A Russian said something in French to the priest who in turn said to me "He says it is the biggest bell in Greece." We all looked up and took in the impressive sight. The bell was decorated with Russian inscriptions and religious images, and I hoped to hear it ring before we left.

As the tour continued we passed an old bent figure who seemed oblivious to us. A schemamonk was looking up at the church as he prayed, his mouth moving silently to the prayers in his heart. In his hand was a long thin prayer rope which he passed through his hand by small movements of his thumb. I was struck by his permanence, the degree to which his life was unchanging while we visitors came and went. I wondered how disruptive our presence was for the monks, and understood how his lack of concern for our presence was the only way he could maintain the life he had left the world for.

The young monk bowed slightly and departed from us, and my thoughts immediately turned to dinner. But my stomach was getting ahead of itself, and as the group moved towards a doorway in the large building opposite the church, I wondered what was happening. We followed behind along a corridor to a stairway of polished stone. Everyone climbed the steps which led to a second floor from which we climbed another stairway. After five floors we were standing outside a large wooden doorway over which was fixed an icon of the Theotokos. Only when we had entered did I realise that this was the church. The monasteries have multiple chapels, but I was surprised to find the top floor of the building being used this way.

It was the largest church interior I had seen on Mount Athos, so large that two lines of seats positioned back to back divided it in half. Around the outside of the room the walls were lined with the same wooden stalls as are found in every Athonite monastery, many of which were now filled with the black shapes of praying monks. Joseph and I followed the flow of pilgrims to the icons standing in front of the iconostasis, and along with everyone else we venerated them. There was a mixture of styles and ages of icons, but almost all of them were elaborately framed and protected with a thick sheet of glass. Along the room were thick square pillars and from these also hung icons before a few of which monks stood praying of bowing in veneration. The high ceiling felt closer because of the many lamps hanging from it, and immediately before the iconostasis hung an elaborate chandelier with countless candles fixed around it.

Joseph and I walked round a group of pillars to look for stalls in which to stand, but they were almost all occupied. We went to the very back of the church and found odd spaces far apart from one another. Leaning back into the wooden frame I felt myself disappear from view into the shadows, and feeling less conspicuous was able to focus on prayer. Hymns were sung by the unseen choir, and the power of their Russian voices was like nothing I had heard before. It was easy to imagine the worship in Moscow as the monks filled the room with praise of God. As I began to say the Jesus Prayer I found my mind filled with thoughts from home and the world, and it took many minutes for me to clear my head and concentrate on what we were doing. As the deacon made his way round the room, the clouds of incense enveloped us, and shafts of light from the windows carved immaterial shapes in the moving air.

The service lasted less than an hour, and as it ended a line of monks began to leave the room. I couldn't see Joseph and decided to find him outside, so I joined the many pilgrims now following the monks out and down the stairs. The evening was still bright and warm, and Joseph was sitting on a wall not far from the doorway.

"That was beautiful," I said unnecessarily.

"Yea, those voices!"

"It's meal time," I said, hoping I was right. A few minutes later a set of doors opened and we were ushered in to the refectory. Long lines of tables were set with dishes of salads, and some kind of pasta dish, and only at seeing the hundreds of plates and dishes laid out did I realise how many people there were looking to be fed. A monk directed me forwards where I was to sit with the other visiting priests amongst the monks. We stood as the abbot prayed, and then pulled out the low benches that ran the length of the tables. Without hesitation everyone began filling their bowls with food, while monks served hot tea from pots they carried down the aisles between us. Everything tasted fresh and good, and the black milkless tea was sweet and strong. Two of the Romanian priests opposite me began chatting in low voices, to which the elderly monk beside me banged his spoon on the table and grumbled in Greek at them: they immediately fell silent. From a stand beside the abbot's table a monk with a half-grey beard began reading aloud in Russian. His voice was deep and purposeful, and carried across the heads of everyone present. Most plates were empty by the time the abbot banged a small hammer to announce the meal was over, and everyone stood once more while he prayed and blessed us. Table by table the room emptied, and I found Joseph once more sitting on the same wall, this time with Father I. who stood when he saw me approaching.

"Father," he said, "we must meet to talk in a little while. I will be around by the trees in about an hour if you have time." He pointed to where he meant as he spoke and I nodded.

"That would be good, Father. We're going to take a little walk first. Do you know if it's okay to go up there?" I pointed to the road that wound round and up past the furthest buildings of the monastery.

"Yes, but don't make any noise near the monks' rooms." He nodded and joined the other visitors heading back to their rooms.

"Are you up to walking after that meal?" I asked Joseph.

"Of course, come on let's see where it goes."

With Joseph leading the way we strolled on past the church and up beyond where we had been able to see. The road broadened out and there were a few cars and trucks parked up out of view. As we continued we met two monks coming towards us, and though they could speak no English, I managed to ask them if we were breaking any rules walking where we were. They waved us on and one of them pulled a face to indicate it was of no concern. As we left the buildings we came to a treeline where the ground looked like it had been prepared for some kind of building work. Beyond the first trees we discovered a small field filled with solar panels, a sign of modern technology that looked at odds with the way of life here. But in reality the use of a clean form of energy made complete sense within a way of life that set out to cause as little harm to the world around it. Thick cables ran back towards the monastery, and the whole set up was a clear indication that the monastery was receiving a good level of financial support. We stood looking out over the reverse view of the monastery, out at sea a small boat was slowly making its way across the horizon; it was a scene that instilled a sense of timelessness and peace. The moment was interrupted as the huge bell tolled its deep call across the monastery. Joseph and I looked at each other, grinning like children at having finally heard it.

As we walked back through the monastery we decided to take a better look round the shop, and as we entered we found it busy with pilgrims. I went through the inner doorway and found myself in a room of large and expensive-looking icons. The gold leaf shimmered all around me, and it was slightly strange seeing these holy objects in the context of a shop. To my right was another doorway which led to an even larger room that stocked vestments and various priestly attire. I strolled past the shelves, admiring the fine stitch work, occasionally reminding myself that it was all beyond my price range. Joseph had followed me in and was admiring a selection of woollen hats that were decorated with different designs. He handed me one bearing a simple cross pattern, "This would suit you," he said.

I tried it on and he smiled his approval. "When would I wear it?" I asked aloud.

"If I could wear it I'd buy it," he said. "When the weather turns cold you'll be glad of it."

I rolled it around in my hands, and since there was little else I could afford, decided it would make a good keepsake from our visit. And of course, it would also give me a chance to pick up one of their carrier bags! I took it to the monk at the counter who looked at the price tag and knocked five euros off. As I paid I felt more like a tourist than a pilgrim, and folded the bag up and hid it in my pocket.

More time had passed than we realised, and as we followed the path back towards our dormitory we saw Father I. sitting where we had agreed to meet. His head was bent forwards and he discreetly passed a prayer rope through his fingers. We approached him silently, not wanting to interrupt his prayers, but as he heard us he smiled in welcome and gestured for us to sit beside him.

"It is an impressive place," he began, "it has been here since the eleventh century."

"The buildings looks so new," I said, "did the original building suffer a fire?"

"The new buildings were built in the nineteenth century, they moved it closer to the sea. There have been many struggles for the monastery to continue, it is a reminder never to lose hope in God. Back in the eighteenth century it was down to only four monks: and now look at how it thrives. We must not be too quick to judge our circumstances by worldly standards, so long as we trust God and try to be faithful, then we know His will will be done. The monastery grew in numbers but nearly a thousand monks were carried away in 1913 over a heretical teaching that those monks had accepted. But good order has now prevailed, and what seemed hard at the time was like a farmer cutting back his fields so that new shoots will grow."

"And it is under Russian control?" I asked

"It is Russian, but all monasteries on the Holy Mountain come under the authority of the Ecumenical Patriarch, since we are, after all, on Athos."

"With so many pilgrims present it was hard to judge how many monks there are here." I said.

"In total there are more than seventy monks here, but not all of them are Russian. There are a few Ukrainians like me. But whatever our nationality, here we are all citizens of the Holy Mountain, because we have died to our old lives." He reached out and held the sleeve of my rassa, "You see this, how black it is, it reminds us that though we are alive, we are dead to the world. Only when we lay down our lives can we truly live. It is not only monks who must put to death some part of themselves, all Christians must do this."

I nodded to his words, and then, as though responding to my feelings of acting like a tourist he said "Prayer is not something we visit, or pick up for some small part of the day. In fact we can say that prayer is not something we just do, it is something we must become. Saint Paul tells us in the New Testament to pray constantly, this is the purpose of our life on Athos, but every Christian must seek to make prayer the foundation of their whole lives. If you are driving your car, or dealing with people at work, all of it must be done prayerfully. We cannot restrict prayer to what we do in our services, our whole being must become a prayer."

"How is this possible?" Asked Joseph.

Father I. looked at him, "We must say the Jesus Prayer, but we must also examine how we have treated other people. At the end of each day we must question our impact on the world. Think about the people we have interacted with, how we have spent our money. Have we been a force for good, have we left our neighbours better off for our having been in the world? Our lives can be a blessing to others and the whole world, but it is a struggle to achieve this. We are selfish, and we feed our passions which strike us as so important. But we can overcome this weakness, look at how many saints have been such a holy impact on the world. This is why we must repent, why we must go to confession. These are like fine surgical tools that help us remove the habits of sin. Of course we are free not to do this, we can live for ourselves and seek every pleasure and comfort that our bodies demand. But the pleasures this brings are an illusion, they are empty, and at some point we come to realise that they are not enough to satisfy our soul. Some people wake up too late, they suddenly see what a waste their lives have been and they face death with nothing to offer for their years. But if we are blessed to glimpse the truth early enough in our lives, then we may choose to put to death this old life so that we can live for God."

"Is this where mysticism fits in Father?" I asked.

"No, not at all." He shook his head, "western ideas of mysticism have nothing to do with Christianity. They are pagan, we must not seek such things. When we humbly give our lives to

God, the sweetness of His presence, the spiritual joys are all too real, but they have nothing to do with the ideas of western mystics. The demons want nothing more than to give us visions and holy feelings, but to accept these things is to throw away our souls. Every one of us must overcome our pride, it is the most dangerous of passions which can quickly lead us to hell. We must not trust in our feelings, our judgement is blinded when the demons take our hand and lead us to such things."

A slight breeze moved the flowers and bushes around us, it prompted me to glance at the sky which was beginning to darken. Father I. was deep in thought, and I wondered if we were keeping him from the little rest he would need before the night service. But any impulse to leave him was pushed aside as he began to speak once more.

"God sometimes allows us to fall, and it is a great blessing for us." He paused for a moment, "You look surprised at this. Listen, when our pride goes unchallenged we can become monsters. But a small fall into sin can make us see our weakness, and may help us to overcome our pride. Without such falls we might become blind to our true condition, and though we must get back up and repent, we should also thank God for those occasions."

"I had never thought to thank God for these things," I admitted.

"We spend so much effort trying not to fall, that when we do our emotions can get the better of us. And our pride can bristle, we can waste the opportunity given to us because we are so stiff necked we feel the artificial picture we have painted of ourselves has collapsed. But when we know ourselves, it comes as less of a shock when we fall, we say to ourselves that it was only to be expected because we know how sick we are, and so we get back into the fight. The demons have many centuries of experience in these matters, they are cunning and know just how to stir up our arrogance. We may be struggling with a sin, and for a short while they withdraw this temptation to convince us we have won that battle. Two things may happen: they may prompt us to feel proud over our great ascetic accomplishment, or they may simply wait until our guard is down. St. Anthony taught that we must struggle to the very last breath, the battle is never over; this life is given that we may be tempered like a blade in a flame. This is the nature of monasticism, to become aware of the constant battle in which we fight, and to understand that only the athlete who runs the race to the very end can taste victory. In all of this it is humility which conquers. We cannot achieve anything without being humble-minded. Above all else I would encourage you to be humble in all things with all people, and flee from anything which brings pride. In this way will we protect our souls from the demons' traps."

I was so caught up in what he was saying that it took me a moment to realise he had stopped speaking. I turned and could see the living evidence of his words: his eyes were as innocent as a child's, but framed in wisdom. Involuntarily I smiled at him, "Thank you," I said.

"It is good to talk a little," he smiled again, "but I must get some rest."

The three of us stood and walked towards the building now half covered in shadow. A few yellow lights had appeared in some of the windows, and as we crossed the metal bridge Father I. wished us goodnight and went down to his room at the other end of the path. Joseph and I quietly descended the steps and at the sink filled our empty water bottles. I read the notice on the wall and was able to figure out that the service began at 3-30am. We let ourselves into our room and kicked off our shoes. As I lay back on the clean sheets the day's events suddenly took their toll on my muscles and I felt that feeling of knowing that sleep was already close. I got to my feet, changed and washed and set the alarm clock to give us thirty minutes to dress and walk to the church. Joseph now had his bedside lamp on and was reading a section of The Philokalia. We exchanged a quick goodnight and almost immediately I was asleep.

Chapter 6

Once more I was woken early by the electronic bleep of my alarm clock. I reached for it as quickly as I could and lay back in the silence. It was impossible to tell if Joseph was still sleeping, so I quietly eased myself out of bed and found my torch. Its beam located my towel and wash bag and I let myself out of the room, still in bare feet. There was no light coming from beneath any of the doors down the corridor as I crept down to the toilets, the only sound being the flop of my feet on the tiled floor. Washed and ready I headed back to our room, feeling like the only person awake on earth. But this thought vanished as the night stillness was replaced with the sound of hammer on wood. Somewhere in the darkness a monk was striking the semantron as he strode around the monastery grounds. His rhythms were steady and practised, and the sense of everyone else sleeping was replaced with the realisation that in the churches all across the mountain, priests were preparing for the Divine Liturgy.

Joseph was up and dressed when I returned, and the sound of the semantron was closer now. We exchanged knowing looks, happy to be hearing what we had listened to together on recordings so many times before. He grabbed his towel and disappeared, while I finished dressing and preparing for the night service. Through the open window I could see moonlight reflected on the black sea, splinters of light in a world possessed by the depth of night. There was plenty of time before the service, but I was impatient to go, and sat watching the door. Eventually Joseph appeared again, and as he came in I saw someone pass by in the shadows of the corridor. "Do you think I'll need my jacket?" He asked.

"No, your jumper will be fine, we won't be outdoors very long."

We locked the room behind us and followed the path towards the large building in the centre of the monastery. Around us in the darkness there were now other pilgrims making the same silent walk to church, and as I glanced into the sky I sensed the whole universe pressing down on us through a cloudless sky. We entered through the large doorway where the black shapes of monks were now joining the flow of bodies towards the stairway. The sound of many feet lightly patting the steps was still the only sound, and as we reached the upper level the yellow glow of candles shimmered either side of the door to the church. A short queue had formed as each man venerated the icons before entering, the golden vision of heaven around Christ moved in waves as the candlelight flickered.

Inside the church there was a lot of activity as pilgrims and monks found their stalls after venerating the images at the front of the church. We moved across in front of the iconostasis where hanging lamps glowed, suspended above our heads by long chains that disappeared into the shadows of the ceiling. There was no movement or sound behind the iconostasis, but to one side candlelight indicated where preparations were taking place. We walked round a large pillar and peered into the darkness, trying to locate vacant stalls. But as we walked towards the back of the church, in each stall we found either a pilgrim or a monk bent over or looking back at us. Finally we found a row of four empty stalls, but by the time we had seated ourselves the other two were also filled. But the flow of pilgrims continued, and the realisation that they were facing a night of standing without support was clearly beginning to sink in as their eyes darted from stall to stall. By the time the small bells of the censor were being shaken there were more than twenty pilgrims standing in small groups, some still scanning the shadows in the hope of a stall that might have been missed.

From our position we could not see the iconostasis, but we could make out the emergence of candlelight as the deacon appeared to begin singing the night office. His voice was a strong tenor which suited the sound of the Russian prayers. But unlike in a Greek service I couldn't identify a single word, and so tried to focus on the act of praying itself. This became easier once the small choir began singing, the verse and response structure is familiar to every Orthodox Christian, regardless of nationality. The tones and mood of the singing was Orthodox in any language, but in

Russian there was an added sense of soberness, there seemed no better national tongue more suited to the serious business of prayer in the night.

As I began to settle myself I found lyrics to secular songs began invading my mind and it took at least half an hour for me to clear my head. It brought home to me how much nonsense I had given my attention to back in the world. Eventually I was able to free myself from the unwanted distractions I had brought with me and I found myself able to pray. I began with the Trisagion prayers but soon settled into the Jesus prayer. Clouds of incense drifted round the church, and the timeless nature of Orthodox worship connected us with God. There were a couple of occasions when everyone removed their headwear, and on one of these I didn't notice it being done. A monk in a stall nearby caught my eye, he pointed to his head and smiled, and nodding my thanks I removed my hat. Before coming to Mount Athos I had been anxious about not knowing how to conduct myself properly and making mistakes like this, but I quickly discovered my fears were groundless; loving acceptance underpins everything the monks do.

There were moments when I glanced around me, and I noticed an old monk to our right turning the plastic pages of an A4 sized folder. At first I assumed he was following the service, but as he turned the next page I noticed columns of names. The book was filled with lists of the names of those who had asked to be prayed for, and here in the shadows a monk was remembering each of them before God. The trust and depth of faith this simple act was filled with struck me deeply, I was left with a renewed sense of the reality of intercessionary prayer. As a consequence I have found it much easier to pray for people simply by naming them before God and knowing that this is as much as is needed. Inspired by this I began naming everyone I knew in the world, and there was a great comfort having them presented before God there on the Holy Mountain.

As the hours passed I noticed a young monk standing before a large icon attached to one of the pillars. He was clearly struggling with exhaustion and as his body began leaning forwards he had to keep holding on to the pillar to prevent himself falling. But despite his body's tiredness he stood and prayed, his will forced him through; he was making a sacrifice in order that his body would submit to his mind. A pilgrim stepped towards him and touched his arm, and silently gestured for the monk to take his stall. But the offer was waved away and the monk returned to his struggle.

As hints of the early morning sun began to appear in the window, the service moved into the Divine Liturgy, and I was able to identify a little more of what was happening. The Gospel was sung in a deep voice that resonated as much as any on an operatic stage. I tried to recall as many of the prayers as I could as the familiar structure of the service carried us forwards, until the priest appeared from the Royal Doors and invited those who were receiving Holy Communion to approach. As in my first visit, I had not spoken to anyone about receiving communion, and so sat back in my stall as a surprisingly small number of the pilgrims joined the few monks who were communicating. As the church began to brighten we could see each other's faces more clearly and the huge number present left me with a strong sense of being anonymous here. But this was mixed with a powerful sense of us being one in our Orthodoxy: the few phrases I had overheard were in Russian and Serbian, but our nationalities were a secondary matter compared with our faith. And the exchange of looks between strangers, and the prayer we shared in, impressed upon us all the single identity we had before God as His Church.

As the choir completed their final hymns the monks began lining up to venerate the icons once more, and the pilgrims joined them. After kissing the last of the icons I turned to look for Joseph but couldn't see him. I left the church and descended the staircase with the other men, all of them continuing to maintain the silence they had entered with. Emerging into the morning sunshine I saw Joseph sitting on the low wall, he gave a small wave to let me know he had seen me.

"Where do we go now?" he asked.

"I'm not sure, let's follow the crowd. It's time for breakfast."

"I'm starving," he added.

After a few minutes the two large wooden doors of the refectory were pushed open and everyone politely entered. Clergy were once more directed to a table amongst the monks, and everyone stood silently behind the long benches. The abbot blessed the food and the air was suddenly filled with the scraping of wood as the benches were simultaneously pulled back so that we could sit. Before us were dishes of tomatoes, olives, potatoes, and a vegetable stew in a thick clear sauce. We heaped the food onto our plates while a young monk served us tea from two huge urns. It was strong and sweet and I savoured every hot drop. In my foolishness I tried to convince myself that to become distracted by the taste of the food was inappropriate, and yet each mouthful was more delicious than the last. The tomatoes must have come straight from Eden, and even the potatoes had a hint of paradise about them. Greed prompted me to take a second helping, but self-consciously I settled for what my plate could hold in a single serving.

After eating I sat with my hands in my lap, aware that I was tired but too content to want to be anywhere else at that moment. The clank of spoons against the metal dishes slowed and eventually stopped altogether, and the abbot rose to his feet. Everyone followed suit and he gave his final blessing. We stepped back over the benches and began moving to the door. To my left I noticed four of the monks who had been serving the tables only now sitting down to eat, and I wondered how long they would be working to clear the tables and wash the dishes. Joseph was standing outside waiting for me, he looked tired.

"Do you want to head back to the room?" He asked.

"Yea, I want to see if I can catch Father I. before we leave. Just to say goodbye."

Joseph nodded, "Okay, I'll see you back there. I'm going to see if I can pick up any more holy souvenirs." We both laughed.

"Right," I said, "I'll see you when you get back."

I watched him for a moment as he followed two monks up some steps, and it occurred to me that there might not be any monks available to open the shop up at this hour. He looked happy to be taking a stroll so I left him to it and headed back towards our room. As I walked I glanced around looking for Father I. amongst the groups now sitting on steps and walls, chatting in low voices, some of them grouped around monks who were answering their questions. As I emerged into an open area alongside a lawn I spotted him sitting alone, as soon as he saw me he smiled and waved. It was clear he had been waiting for us, and even before I reached him he began to call over to me.

"I wanted to speak with you before you left," he said. "How did you find the service?"

"It was very beautiful."

"Yes," he nodded, "Russian choirs are outstanding. Even in a monastery Russians always find good singers." There was a sense of pride in his words that was well deserved, and though he was Ukrainian, I could see how closely he identified himself with his Russian neighbours.

"How is your Russian?"

"Not so good," he admitted, "I have to think hard before speaking. But for the Liturgy I have no problem in any language. Prayer is the same whatever words we use, if our hearts are united and offered to God, then our lips only have to be the servants. Do you know what I mean by this?"

"Yes, I felt it too, even as a visitor."

"No," he waved his hand, "you come here as a brother in Christ. The monks do not see themselves as the owners of this place, they do not possess it. When you come here, even if it is only once in your lifetime, it is as a much yours as theirs. And in truth, none of us own Athos, it belongs to the Mother of God. She visited the peninsula and loved it so much God gave it to her protection. We work the land and toil over our hearts, but every drop of sweat that falls from our brows is offered to her. And she goes on protecting us through her prayers. She holds us before her Son. This is why the air is so heavy with our prayers here, we pray in her garden, and every breath we take she gives to us. How can we, who have been permitted to spend our years here, imagine it is ours to keep? We are all guests of the Mother of God, every one of us."

He pointed to a wooden bench, "Do you have time to talk a little more?"

"Yes, thank you."

We sat facing the lawn, across the path from us was yet another immaculate flower bed full of colour. An early morning breeze blew across our faces but already the day was warming. Reflecting the sunlight his piercing blue eyes looked sharper than ever, I was aware of the intelligence behind them.

"When you return to the world, you must try to take with you something of Mount Athos. I do not mean the stones or the trees, but the way of life here, the prayer. A visit is good, but it is better if it flavours the rest of your days."

"I hope I do that," I admitted, "but it isn't easy."

"You are right, it isn't easy, because the whole world is working against us. Societies are being organised to suppress our faith, businesses make money trying to distract us from our purpose. It is not easy at all, but the difficulty of the task only makes it more precious."

"What practical things do you suggest Father?"

He thought for a moment, "You must create good habits. Even a tiny good habit can change your soul. Just as tiny bad habit can lead us to hell." He looked out into the distance once more, deep in thought, then continued "Saint John Chrysostom warns us that the worst kind of tyranny a man can suffer is a bad habit. Do you know why this is?"

"Because it is difficult to overcome? I suggested.

"More than that, it is because the smaller a bad habit appears to us, the less we even try to overcome it. Saint John tells us that we even accept some and don't repent of them at all. We tell ourselves we would never murder, or commit adultery, or any of those other big sins, but then we happily look away when we see these little, inconsequential sins which we allow ourselves every day. They may be thoughts, they may be actions, but unless we struggle against them they can transform our very soul. It is tyranny because we become enslaved, we give away our liberty when we choose habits of sin: we exchange our liberty for what the devil has to offer. This is a serious business because we are created in God's image to be free. Everything we do in life is only truly free when sin is absent. If we allow the passions to rule us then we are shackled and bound. But we do not see the chains when they are first placed on our feet, they are so light, so small, we consider them as nothing. Only if we try to break free do we learn how heavy these chains are, and how surely we are enslaved."

He turned to look me in the eye, "But what the demons know can also be used against them. We are creatures of habit. They know how to entrap us, how to cultivate bad habits in us. But good habits have the opposite effect. When we build habits of good thought and action into our daily lives, it makes it harder for the demons to trip us up. Good habits are essential. If we rely on doing good only when we feel like it, or praying only when we feel inspired to pray, what good can come of it? No, we must pray when we don't want to pray, repent when we feel like doing evil. We can only do this by building habits into our lives that don't rely on what we want." He smiled, "After all, if we felt like doing good all the time we'd already be saints."

"I understand about building a pattern of prayer, but how do we develop good habits in other ways?"

His smile broadened, "I once knew a married couple who forgot how to smile at one another. Can you believe that, they never exchanged a smile for many years? He came to me one day and I told him to fake it for the good of his wife. It sounds terrible, to fake a smile, but every day he forced himself to smile at her, and do you know, in a short time she began smiling back. Soon their life together changed, and he didn't have to fake his smiles anymore. This is how we must behave, we must force ourselves to do what is needed to help people around us. A smile can be a great healer for someone who is alone and feels that no one cares. Or a kind word, or to let someone know we are grateful for what they do. We make sure that every day we treat at least one person with kindness, even if it means going out of our way. This will soften our hearts, and with time, being kind will come naturally to us because we will have changed the condition of our heart. Just as evil can distort our soul, so doing good can help us to heal. Of course, it is no good just doing good, we must do all things for Christ, treat our neighbour as a representative of Christ, so that our actions are not empty. If we believe that every man is created in God's image, then we must honour His image in each other. The demons hate mankind because they hate God, and they see His likeness in us. We must see His likeness too, and as Christians value what is most precious. But I must qualify what I have said about habits. Many saints remind us that prayer can never be a habit like these other things, because it is the thing that the demons will try to prevent us from doing above all else. Prayer must be a daily struggle, something we must make an act of will about 'till the day we die."

As he was speaking Joseph walked down the path towards us, in his hand was a small paper bag from the shop. I made room for him on the bench and he sat beside me. We acknowledged one another before Father I. added "One of the most important habits to develop is discernment. We must train ourselves to look carefully at what is before us and recognise its true purpose and effect. If we are watching television, we must consciously ask ourselves what the programme maker intended to make us feel, what it is that is being stirred up within us as we watch it. We must learn to keep guard of our senses, so that the demons don't have access to us. They use everything they can, and we often allow them in unchecked, but we must treat our eyes, our ears, all of our senses, as doorways to our souls. We must choose what to let in, and reject what is not welcome."

"There are a lot of things on my course at university that are dangerous," said Joseph. "Some of the lectures are just liberal garbage, full of political opinions."

"But you know this," said Father I. "you see what is being taught for what it is. As long as you remain aware you will not be harmed by it." I turned to look at Joseph and saw in his face a look of fixed concentration, he was hearing something very real to him

"When you leave here," Father I. continued, "remember how sweet it feels to pray. Even when that sweetness isn't there, remember it, so that some part of you will look for it again. And take the sound of silence with you, not just the absence of noise, but the stillness that comes from a world dedicated to God. This is the silence that nothing can take from you. You can visit a big city, but this silence will remain. This is an important habit to develop, the practice of stillness."

Joseph and I nodded, "Thank you Father," I said softly. "What are you going to do next?"

He pulled an amused expression, "I am not sure, I must speak to the abbot, but it will be alright for a little while, until the future is more clear. But I know it is in God's hands, and whatever He gives us we must receive gratefully. Even if it is not what we want."

With so much uncertainty hanging over him it felt awkward to just get up and walk away. But there was nothing we could do to affect his situation and I got to my feet. "Father, it has been such a blessing for us to meet you. Thank you again for your time and words." I reached into my pocket and found one of our printed parish cards with my contact details on it, "Please take this, if there's anything I might be able to help with do get in touch."

He took the card and studied it carefully, "I have a card too." He rummaged around inside his rassa and pulled out a bent card covered in a script I didn't recognise. He then found a pen and started adding more text: "I will write my details down for you."

He handed it to me, and I said "Which path do we follow to get to Daphne?"

"Ah yes," he turned towards the path rising up into the trees to our right, "follow that path and it will take you all the way."

"How long do you think it will be to walk?" I asked.

"Oh, no more than two hours I should think, it is a good path."

This was reassuring news, and I thanked him. We embraced and kissed, and it hardly seemed possible that we had only known him for such a short period of time. We exchanged goodbyes and in silence Joseph and I followed the path back to our room. Once inside I enquired about Joseph's package and he pulled out a fridge magnet showing a picture of the monastery. It was funny to see such an item here on the Holy Mountain, but I was pleased he had bought it. We collected our things and straightened the room as best we could. We left the room key on the inside of the door as directed, and with no official process of leaving required, we filled our water bottles and left.

Chapter 7

We climbed the hill leaving the monastery, constantly stopping to look back and take in the view that was expanding as we got higher. We could now see more of the green onion domes nestled in amongst the many roofs, a small piece of Russia hiding amongst the arid hills of Greece.

"We're out of the monastery grounds now," I observed, "let's take some pictures." The usually camera-shy Joseph happily posed for me with the incredible scene behind him, he knew how special this place was. As we messed around with the camera a huge golden dog approached us. I had read warnings about the dogs that can be encountered on the continent, but Joseph didn't share my wariness, he crouched low and held out his hand. The animal stepped closer and sniffed at him, but wasn't going to get near enough to be patted. He stood staring at us, as though waiting to be fed.

"What i̵s̵ ̵i̵t̵?" Joseph asked.

"Some kind of mongrel, his coat looks like there's some golden retriever in him, but look at the size of him."

"He seems friendly, do you think he belongs to the monastery?"

"He must belong to someone, he couldn't survive out here and look so healthy if no one was looking after him."

We set off once more along the path, and before long Joseph said "Look, he's following us."

"I hope he doesn't come too far, he might get lost."

We walked on for a few minutes past some driverless bulldozers and an area of ground that looked like it was being prepared for more building work. "Maybe he belongs to the workmen," I suggested. The path continued to rise until, after about ten minutes of walking we reached the first crest and were able to look down at the sea on the other side. We could see how the coast meandered in and out of small bays, but as yet there was no view of Daphne or the other monastery we had to pass before reaching the port. The dog continued to follow us a few strides back, and each time we stopped he did too. His tail occasionally wagged, but mostly he assumed a placid, almost disinterested attitude.

By now my bag was beginning to cut into my shoulder, and every few minutes I had to stop to adjust its position. Beneath the meagre shade of a tall tree we stopped once more.

"What did you think of the monastery?" I asked.

"Obviously it was an amazing place, but…"

I wasn't sure if his hesitation was over how to word his answer or whether or not he should express how he felt. So I jumped in, "It was a little impersonal wasn't it."

97

"Yea, it would have been good to speak to the monks perhaps, but it was so big, and there were so many visitors."

"I felt the same," I admitted, "but if they spent their time talking to pilgrims they might as well have stayed in the world. This is their life, they've come here to escape the world, and they have to be careful we don't bring too much of the world into their lives."

Joseph nodded, and I knew I wasn't saying anything he didn't already know. To encourage him I added "The next one is much smaller. You'll get a different impression." Saying this I realised a part of me was interpreting our experiences from a selfish perspective, with set expectations. I tried to shake them off and accept whatever came with a greater openness, so that I was less likely to ignore what God might be leading us to.

Joseph helped position my bag and we walked on. After a while the path snaked along the edge of a steep cliff, at the bottom of which ran a stream that was somehow finding enough water up in the dry hills to make it all the way down here to the sea. We followed the path round and came to a beautiful bridge built of white stone, it was a magical sight, a sign of enormous care and work. We sat for a moment on one of its walls, and watched the stream running beneath us. The bridge was a long way from any monastery, and yet as much care had been taken over its construction and maintenance as any structure in the middle of the monasteries. It brought home how the whole of

Mount Athos is treated with great respect by the monks, even a dusty path surrounded by bushes and rocks. We walked a little further and the two cliffs opened up on either side to frame the blue of the Aegean Sea, a calm mass of colour matched only by the cloudless sky above it. Without saying anything we stood staring at it, the beauty of the physical environment of the Holy Mountain exceeding anything a photograph or video could convey. As we stood there the dog appeared once more, and nonchalantly trotted past us as though we weren't there.

"He looks like he knows where he's going," I said hopefully, still worried that we might have helped him to get lost.

After another forty minutes I began to struggle with my bag and was requesting to stop more frequently. No doubt a little frustrated by our rate of progress, Joseph picked up my bag and swung it over his back with his own.

"What are you doing?" I exclaimed.

"Come on, it's fine, if it gets too heavy I'll give it back to you." And without another word he strode ahead and I was left following in his trail. It was a moment of realisation for me. A few years before I had walked for nearly five hours between monasteries, and now I was being helped by my son. It wasn't just a matter of fitness, I was growing old. But I was happy to see my son's youth and strength; that phase of life was now his, and knowing this more than made up for what time was doing to me.

We came to a handmade wooden sign-post that indicated we were close to the next monastery, and I was keen for Joseph to see it as we would be coming back here for our final night. I also wanted to see again the first monastery I had visited when I came on my original trip. But the path cut down towards the sea and away from the monastery, and though I was disappointed, we were grateful to be walking downhill and to allow gravity to assist us. A little further we joined a wide dirt road along which trucks and buses had left their tracks. As we walked Joseph suddenly shouted in alarm "Snake!" He jumped away from the embankment, and pointed towards the bushes. "There," he shouted, "look, it's huge." The genuine concern in his voice was mixed with excitement.

I rushed over but couldn't see it, "What colour was it?"

"Black, all black, it was huge, really long. I didn't know there are snakes like that here. Do you think it's poisonous?"

"I don't know, but we probably disturbed it having a sleep in the sun." I took hold of his arm and guided him further away from the bushes, "Let's stay in the middle of the road just in case." Joseph didn't need convincing, but he was clearly glad to have seen it. "Be careful how you tell your mother about this," I grinned, "she won't let me hear the end of it if she thinks I've put you at risk of snake bites." Joseph laughed as we both followed a line as far from the two hedgerows as we could.

From somewhere behind us we heard an engine approaching and stepped off the road to allow it to pass. "Be careful when it comes," I warned him, "some of the drivers here will give you a bigger fright than that snake." Again he laughed, and as the sound drew closer we stood motionless, waiting for it to pass. Around the bend came a green four wheeled truck with two young monks in the cabin. As it drew closer I waved and smiled, and one of the monks waved back. But instead of passing us, it slowed and stopped, and the passenger wound down his window to ask "Daphne?"

"Yes," I nodded, realising our trek was coming to an end.

He pointed to the seats behind them, "Get in," he said.

We pulled open the door and slid across the seat, "Thank you," I said, leaning forwards slightly, "it was getting warm."

There wasn't a hint of grey in either of their long beards, I guessed they were in their mid to early thirties. Without exchanging a further word with us or one another, and at a surprisingly steady speed they followed the road down to Daphne. The port came into sight as a flash of orange rooves and white stone, and as we approached we could see crowds of men milling around. I had never seen the place so busy, and I hoped it was a sign that the ferries would be arriving soon. The truck pulled up just before the buildings, and we thanked them again. What had been just ten minutes as passengers would have been another forty minutes on foot. Instead of arriving exhausted we were refreshed from sitting in the shaded vehicle, and this renewed our enthusiasm for what Daphne had to offer.

To our right was a wall on which sat a large crowd of lads aged no more than thirteen or fourteen, all of them in rassas. It was a curious sight, but their relaxed manner gave the impression they were perfectly used to being there. They chatted and laughed like any group of boys that age, and some of them eagerly ate pastries they had bought from Daphne's café. Along the foot of the wall were their bags, and it was obvious they had come for at least a few days. The white stone of the short pier jutted out into the sea behind them, where piles of bags sat waiting for the ferry to return.

To our left was a covered patio on which small tables and chairs had been set out: they were almost all being used by customers. Seeing the coffee cups and plates of food Joseph's thoughts turned to his own stomach. "Are you hungry?" He asked.

"No, I'm okay, do you want some money?"

"No, I've got plenty, I'll see you in a minute."

He disappeared into the shade of the café and as I prepared to wait for him I noticed a water tap fixed to the wall where two young men were filling their bottles. I waited for them to finish and then did the same, even splashing a little onto my face. I leaned against the wall and took a drink, nothing on earth tastes better than water when you've been walking in the heat. As I looked around I spotted a few cats stretched out near the café tables, their open wide eyes watching every morsel of food around them. Just then I spotted the golden dog that had been following us. He had walked by himself all the way to Daphne, and was now pacing up and down the main road begging for food. As he approached a few of the cats he sniffed at them but they ignored him. There I had been worrying about him getting lost when in reality he knew exactly where he was going. He hadn't been following us at all, we had just been in his way. Joseph emerged with something wrapped in paper and a can of coke, "What have you got?" I asked.

"Some kind of pastry, it looks good. It was quite cheap too."

"Look," I pointed, "it's the dog."

Joseph smiled, "He's covered some miles."

"I need to buy tickets for the ferry round to Gregoriou," I said, "do you want to sit on the wall and wait?"

"Yea, I'll see you in a minute. Give me your bag." He strolled over and sat amongst the other pilgrims, while I walked to the little window where the tickets were sold. There was a small queue, but everything went smoothly and the man serving us knew how to be efficient. He handed me the two little stubs and then vanished into the shadows of his room. As I turned to find Joseph I noticed the ferry coming into sight as it followed the shape of the coastline. I found our bags but Joseph was nowhere to be seen. In any other foreign location I would have been nervous, but on Athos I had no concerns. I scanned the crowd but couldn't see him, and so sat up on the wall where he had been before. Next to me sat two young men speaking in Greek, "Excuse me," I said in my typically English approach, "do you know if that is the ferry going to Gregoriou?"

In good English but with a strong Greek accent the man nearest me threw a glance over his shoulder at the approaching ferry and said "Yes, it will leave in ten minutes."

"Thank you," I said.

"You are from England?" He asked.

"Yes, I'm here with my son."

"I visited London when I was at school, I liked it very much."

"I've only been to London a few times," I said, "I'm not really one for big cities."

"But London has many old buildings, there is a lot to do there."

"Yes that's true, where are you from?"

"We are from Thessaloniki," he pointed to his friend.

"That must make it easy for you to visit Athos," I said, "how often do you come?"

"We have been coming every year at least once since we were about seventeen, some years we have come very often, but it has been difficult to find so much time lately. It has been nearly a year since our last visit. Have you been to Gregoriou before?"

"Yes, this is only my second visit, but I wanted to make sure I went back there."

"I understand," he smiled, "we only visit Gregoriou, every question we wish to ask can be answered there. I hope you have a blessed visit."

The ferry was nearing the port, it was the same low, flat design of the one we had ridden the day before, but about two thirds the size. The two Greek men climbed down from the wall and offered their hands to me for a blessing. I slipped down and blessed them both, still humbled by the experience of strangers kissing my hands. There was a general movement towards the pier, but Joseph was still nowhere to be seen. I strained to find him, anxious that we might miss our ride. The front of the ferry was lowered and the men began to step forward to offer their tickets. I watched as they began climbing up to the upper deck, wishing I was with them. There was a squeeze of my arm and I turned to find Joseph behind me, "Have you got the tickets?"

"Where have you been?" I tried not to let my irritation show.

"I was in the shops, they've got some incredible icons. Will we have time to visit them on our way back?"

"Definitely," I assured him, "come on, let's get aboard."

We trotted over to wait behind behind the few pilgrims still on the pier, and once we had stepped onto the iron deck I relaxed. A man seated at a small table glanced at our tickets before handing them back to us, and we walked along the length of the boat to climb the steps. Even before we had made it to the upper deck, we felt the shudder of the engines coming to life and felt the ferry begin to reverse away from Daphne.

Chapter 8

The clear blue waves rolled and frothed along the hull of the ferry as it reversed out into the sea. Once the captain was happy he had swung round far enough we felt the jolt as the boat lurched forwards away from Daphne. There were no seats left on the top deck, but in the intense sunshine we were happy to drop our bags and lean against the metal rails to watch as the coastline of Athos revealed itself. I spotted the pathway I had followed on foot three years before and was surprised at the distance I had walked.

The ferry turned round the first outcrop of the coastline and within a few minutes Daphne was out of sight. Perched on the arid hillside we spotted small hermitages and began to imagine the lives of prayer there. Around them were small vegetable gardens, patches of dark green cultivated from the dry yellow ground. As the ferry moved on we saw more trees, and even small natural woodlands, punctuated by the occasional hermitage.

I pointed out the pathway and told Joseph "That's the path I followed."

He nodded as he studied my route, no doubt realising I would not have made it in my present shape.

As we made our way along the coastline the peak of Mount Athos constantly loomed above us. Its high triangular shadow still streaked with rivulets of ice imposed a sober mood on everyone who looked at it. Its presence spoke of a permanence that mortal men could not comprehend, a reminder of our transience and the fleeting nature of all our concerns. But even this vast monument to time is as nothing to the eternity prepared for by the monks and all Christians. Its shadow against the light of the day also reminded us of the hidden struggles seen only by God that were performed all across the peninsula.

The cliffs grew higher and now there was only a dense shrubbery that clung low to the ground above the steep edge of the land. But as the ferry rounded another outcrop we could see the pale shape of Simona Petras looking as though it had not been built by men, but had emerged from the rock, called out by God to shelter the monks. As we grew closer we could make out four rectangular blocks of buildings, each marked with lines of dark windows. Below the monastery at the water's edge was the small pier and boat house towards which the ferry began to turn. As we drew closer and our speed reduced the ferry began to rock violently from side to side. We continued to draw closer to the pier but the rocking continued, and I estimated how far the jump would be if we felt the boat was going over. I glanced around and saw alarm on a number of men's faces; at least it wasn't just me getting nervous.

But as we reached the pier and slowed to a stop, the ferry steadied itself, and through the lowered bow a handful of pilgrims headed towards the steep climb ahead of them. I looked up and Simona Petras was now silhouetted against the cloudless sky, as imposing as any castle.

No one boarded and in less than two or three minutes the bow was lifted and we were reversing once more. Again the rocking motion began, and I tried to assure Joseph everything was alright.

"We're getting the worst of it because we're so high up," I explained, "it's probably nowhere near as bad on the lower deck." Joseph grinned back at me, a look of fearlessness in his face as he enjoyed the ride.

We felt the now familiar shift of gear and the ferry manoeuvred out to continue its journey once more. Almost immediately we could see the Monastery of Saint Gregoriou, looking as if it was sitting on the water. I felt a rush of excitement to see it again, though I had never seen it from the sea before. Next to the main building was a white harbour wall that ran the length of a small bay. There were two and three storey buildings made of the same white stone with the standard Greek orange tiled roof lining the far end of the pier.

"Let's get down to the front," I said, and we lifted our bags and descended the steps. The side of the ferry giving a view of the peninsula was crowded as everyone got the best sight of Athos, so we slipped along the starboard side without any difficulty. As we did so the rocking began once more, and just as violently. But being lower in the water we felt its effect less, although I was concerned about two trucks parked on deck and wanted to get past them as quickly as possible in case they began sliding towards us. We joined a group of around ten men looking over the bow at the monastery approaching. The sun shimmered on its yellow stone giving it an unearthly glow as it nestled amongst some trees. The grind of the gears vibrated through the hull and one of the crew lowered the bow. The ferry was still moving slightly and the iron gate scraped loudly along the stone. We hopped out onto land and everyone immediately began walking towards an incline paved in rounded stone slabs. Along its edges were smooth pathways and two lines of men formed as we climbed up towards the walls of the monastery. By the time we had reached half way the groups had strung out according to everyone's different level of fitness: some strode on without pausing, while others did it in stages needing stops to catch their breath. We looked back at the ferry as it pulled away to continue on around the end of the peninsula, on to a side of Athos I had not yet encountered.

The path emerged onto an enclosed walkway which led to a beautiful arched gateway. Through the archway we found ourselves in a whitewashed open ended building, almost like a gatehouse. On its pristine walls hung huge framed icons of saints I didn't recognise, and my Greek wasn't sufficient to translate their names. Beyond this was a small courtyard, lined with immaculate flower beds, and at the far end was a stone structure inside of which we could see a large stone font. As beautiful as the monastery was, above all it felt very human. There was nothing austere or overly grand, everything looked welcoming and even homely.

We followed the footpath through another arch into the central square of the monastery. Other than the newly arrived pilgrims there was no movement or sound, and as we entered we found a small group wondering which way they should go. I pointed to their right, up a flight of stone steps which led to a long balcony, "The guest master's room is up there," I said.

As we climbed the steps I stopped to look back at the courtyard. Immediately before us was the low roof of the church, and outside the church hung a large bent loop of iron with a hammer dangling beside it. The square was surrounded by grey roofed buildings, each with a small red tiled shelter that hung out over the yard. The floor consisted of patterned slabs surrounding an octagon of multi-coloured stone, and positioned near the walls were large flower pots with carefully shaped bushes growing nearly to the level of the roofs. The subtle level of ornamentation prevented anything from appearing harsh, but nothing looked feminine. Even the doorways to the church had had stone archways built in front of them, giving ordinary rectangular entrances a look of antiquity.

The other pilgrims were now speaking to a small, middle aged monk who slowly spoke to each in turn in an unflustered manner. As Joseph and I approached he turned to us, "Hello Father," he said, "do you have a reservation?"

"Yes, Spyridon and Joseph."

"Please follow me," he said before disappearing into his office. We found ourselves in a whitewashed room decorated only with three icons on the wall behind a large desk. He found his clipboard and ran his finger down a sheet of paper, "Ah yes," his Greek accent was strong but he was confident in his use of English, "please take a seat outside for a moment and I will be with you shortly."

Immediately outside his office was a large sink where two of the other visitors were refilling their bottles. We waited and then did the same, happy to be able to sit on the long wooden bench and sip at the cold water. The monk walked passed us with his clip board, and one of the other pilgrims approached us.

"Have you made a reservation Father?"

"Yes," I said, "and you?"

"No, none of us have." His accent was French, but the hopeful tone in his voice was unmistakeable in any language. "Do you think they will have room for us?"

"I don't know," I admitted, "they seemed busy when I booked. It all depends who's turned up."

He smiled and pointed at a room to our left, "If they'll let us we'll camp down in there for the night."

I was surprised that they had made the trip without arranging where they would stay, and though our accommodation was assured, I felt slightly anxious for them. "What will you do if they can't fit you in?"

"I suppose we will have to walk to the next monastery and try there."

"I know they're full at Simona Petras," I said, "I tried to book us in quite a while ago."

His smile faded as the reality of his predicament began to sink in. "We will trust in God," he said.

"Are you Orthodox?"

"No," he shook his head and there was an almost apologetic look on his face, "we are Roman Catholic, but very interested in Orthodoxy."

"Is this your first visit to Athos?" I asked.

"Yes, we drove from Paris to get here."

"You drove all the way?" I was surprised at this, "where's your car?"

"We left it at the side of the road just outside Ouranoupolis, I hope it is still there when we get back."

His smile was open and warm, and I was impressed with his determination to be here. He looked passed me and I turned to see the guest master returning. Still looking at his papers he said to the Frenchman "We will be able to take care of you. Please take a seat, it will be a little while to prepare your rooms." There was an evident relief amongst the whole group, and they happily began moving to the benches. He glanced my way and we nodded relief at each other. The monk looked at us,

"Father Spyridon, Joseph, would you come with me please."

We followed him to the floor above us where we found ourselves on a long corridor along which framed icons hung between the rooms. The floor was a dark polished wood, and despite the many rooms it would have been impossible to mistake it for a hotel. At our door he handed me the key and smiled warmly, "Have you been here before?"

"Yes, a few years ago. It's good to be back. Will it be alright if we receive Holy Communion tomorrow?"

"Yes, of course, you are Orthodox. It is Sunday tomorrow so the whole community will receive communion."

"Is there someone I should notify or approach first?"

"No, don't worry about a thing, I will let them know. There is a service in two hours, you will hear a bell."

"Thank you, is it alright if we wander around until then?"

"Of course," he made a small bow and headed back to try and sort out his unexpected guests. We let ourselves in to the little room which contained the usual two single beds, a desk and a wardrobe. Above the head of the beds were exquisite icons of Christ and the Theotokos, and opposite the door was a window with a deep sill. I strode over and pulled the window open, and found myself looking out over one of the squares we had walked through. From above the sense of order was only reinforced, and as I stood leaning on the sill a soft breeze found its way in.

"Do you want to take a look around?" I asked Joseph.

"I do, but I wouldn't mind having a nap first."

"I'm the same," I said, "just half an hour to recover."

I hung my rassa on the back of the door, pulled off my trousers and lay them in front of the window in the hope that the combination of breeze and sun would air them, and then lay out on top of the sheets. Joseph was setting the alarm on his 'phone, "Is half an hour long enough?" He asked.

"Give it forty minutes," I suggested, and almost immediately we were both sleeping.

Chapter 9

I woke a few minutes before the alarm went off. The air in the room was cool but still warm enough for my uncovered legs to feel comfortable. I turned towards Joseph and could see the steady rise and fall of his chest as he slept. From beyond our window there was silence, I strained to listen but the stillness was unbroken. Not even birds or the wind made a sound, the tumult of the world was far away. I tried to take in where we were, almost as though I was trying to force my mind to capture the reality of the experience. It all felt too precious to allow a failing memory to be the only contact I would have with this moment. But then catching myself like this I understood that my concern for perhaps one day not remembering all the details was disrupting the moment itself. I tried to let go of such foolishness, and allow the peace of the monastery to envelop me. I began to run my prayer rope through my fingers, and immediately understood why we were there. The beauty and peace of the place weren't the goal, they were part of the means of drawing closer to God. The only thing that mattered was that when we returned to our ordinary lives, we continued to seek God with the hunger that Athos inspires.

Joseph's alarm began to beep, he had set it to a low volume so as not to disturb anyone, and with very little body movement, his arm swung out and he turned it off. There was silence for a moment, and then he rolled on to his side to face me.

"Do you feel better?" I asked.

"Yea, I needed that. It's so peaceful here."

"I know, what do you think of the monastery?"

"I felt at home as soon as we walked through the gate," he smiled, "I love it here."

I was happy to hear him say what I was feeling too. "The services will make that feel stronger," I assured him.

"It's not just the quiet though, everything here feels…" His sentence trailed off, but he didn't need to find the words.

"It just feels right, doesn't it?"

He nodded and hesitated. "I had a dream."

"What about?" I asked.

"I dreamed a monk was leading us through the sea like Moses."

He studied my face for a response, but I couldn't think what to say. In the end I settled for "It might just be your mind dealing with all that's going on," but secretly it struck me as significant.

I swung my feet out over the edge of the bed and leaned my elbows on my knees, "Do you want to have a wander round before the service?"

"Definitely," he said, climbing to his feet.

I reached up to my trousers and found they were fresh and dry, and it was a relief to be wearing clothes that weren't damp with sweat. As I pulled on my rassa I noticed a hand-written sign stuck to the back of the door. "DO NOT LEAVE VALUABLES IN YOUR ROOM AND LOCK IT WHEN YOU LEAVE. THERE ARE SOME PILGRIMS WHO COME TO ATHOS TO STEAL." It was disappointing to read, and I called Joseph over to see it.

"That's a real shame," was all he said.

Beyond the main courtyard was a narrow street beside which climbed high buildings, their wooden balconies perfectly positioned to catch the evening sun. We retraced our steps and found our way back to the outdoor font. Inside its shelter were large icons of various biblical scenes linked to water, all painted in vibrant colours.

"When Alan visited Mount Athos he wasn't Orthodox," Joseph said. "I don't know which monastery he went to, but they offered to baptise him, but he wanted to wait until he was home so that Father D. could do it. I think he's glad he chose that, but imagine being baptised here."

"It's not big enough to stand in," I observed, "they must pour plenty of water from a bowl or something."

Above our heads was a wooden terrace along which vines were growing. There wasn't a dying or shrivelled plant anywhere, which seemed a wonder in such a dry environment. There was no one about so I furtively took a few photographs of Joseph beside the icons, at least I had something to show his mother when we returned. There was still a little time before we were due in church so we found a wall to sit on that overlooked the sea. The previous day's mists had completely disappeared and the Aegean had returned to its light turquoise as it gently lapped the shore. We sat quietly for a while, content to allow the surroundings to affect us.

After a while I said "How long have we got?"

He looked at his 'phone, "The service starts in fifteen minutes."

"I'd like to get in church early, is that okay with you?"

"Yea, of course," he nodded.

"With so many pilgrims it might be a squeeze."

It took our eyes a moment to adjust to the low light of the church as we entered, and it was only after we had venerated the first set of icons that I noticed the bent figure of a monk sitting in the shadows to our left. It was impossible to tell if he was watching us or if his head was bent in prayer. We passed through the heavy doors to where there were more dark stalls, almost all of them empty except for a couple of pilgrims who were looking at the frescoes around them. I waved Joseph on to the final set of interior doors which were already open, and we found ourselves before the imposing iconostasis. Much of it was golden, its icons darkened from so many years of candle smoke. Joseph slid into one of the stalls at the back, and as I was about to follow him a monk appeared at my side.

"Father, please sit here." He pointed to the stalls immediately beside the iconostasis, and I found myself sitting in the very same place as on my previous visit. Some of the choir had already gathered, and over the next few minutes I found myself surrounded by the black robed figures as they quietly took their seats. To my left I saw a monk I recognised, he was now a schemamonk, the red embroidered cross beneath his exorasson indicating a level of austerity and self-renunciation that even the ordinary monks consider a special calling.

I sat looking at the face of the Theotokos, everything here was her treasure and I felt a great sense of gratitude for everything around me that she made possible. As I tried to focus on these thoughts the deacon emerged swinging the censor, and clouds of rose scented incense curled around the pillars and candle stands. Above us was an enormous candelabra on which he lit one of the candles. Without any obvious cue the choir began to sing the office, their strong voices moving back and forth across the church as two groups sang the verses and responses. An older monk calmly found each of the books as it was needed and lay the opened pages before the singers. Standing in their midst I felt the power of their intention; here everything was directed towards God, and the structure of their daily lives was focussed on these times of worship. From behind the iconostasis the priest's voice led the prayers in a solemn offering, a sound that has been heard on Mount Athos for over a thousand years.

The hour passed quickly, and the monks began to file forwards to venerate the icons. One of them gently gripped my elbow to lead me forwards, and as I kissed the icon of Christ I understood that there was nothing on earth more important than what was happening here. As I walked through the church in the line of monks I saw Joseph now approaching the iconostasis with the other pilgrims and I was surprised at how many there were. We continued out into the sunshine and immediately beside the church, wide doors were now open to allow us into the refectory. By now I knew I would be guided to sit amongst the monks, but it felt presumptuous to just take my place amongst them, and I hesitated a little. But straightaway a monk ushered me forwards and I stood at the table beside the silent black figures. Before us were dishes of vegetables, pasta, bread, fruit and a dark soup. They triggered a sense of hunger that up until now I hadn't been aware of. The abbot said the prayers and we crossed ourselves and sat to eat. Everything was fresh and delicious, a different kind of taste to anything bought in a supermarket. As we ate one of the monks read aloud from a spiritual text, but the Greek was completely impenetrable to me; the clank of cutlery on the metal dishes was the only other sound.

The meal ended with the abbot's prayer and we walked out into the sunshine. Small groups of pilgrims were standing and sitting with monks, there was no sense of them disappearing to their cells to avoid their visitors. As Joseph approached me I spotted the monk I had spent hours speaking to on my last visit, and I was keen for Joseph to meet him. As his conversation with two young Greek men came to an end I stepped forwards.

"Father D.," I said, "I visited the monastery a few years ago and we talked."

My heart sank as I saw a complete lack of any recognition in his face. Meeting him had meant so much to me, and my hope was that Joseph would have the same opportunity on this trip. But in a guileless manner Father D. shook his head and said "I don't remember."

"That's alright, I just wanted to let you know that the things you said to me had a profound effect, I'm very grateful to you."

He smiled, "Good, thank you."

We walked away and back to our room, Joseph could sense my disappointment. "It doesn't matter whether we get to speak to one of the monks, being here is enough."

"I know," I said, only half agreeing, "but it was one of the most important parts of my pilgrimage." As we slumped across our beds, I recognised how my desire to repeat the good experience that I had had before was in danger of distracting me from what this pilgrimage had to offer. I pushed my disappointment to one side, and thought about the service.

"What did you think of their singing?" I asked.

"It was completely different to the Russians, it didn't have the same power, but I preferred it."

"I know what you mean, I felt that too. Even though it was in Greek, it just felt more accessible if that sounds right."

"Yea, exactly," he said, "relaxed isn't the right word either, but it was less imposing." He paused for a moment, and then as he lay on his back, almost speaking to the ceiling, he said "I love this monastery."

"It's worth trying to get some sleep, we've got another long night ahead of us."

"I'm ready now," he said, "it must be the sea air."

He pulled off his jeans and slid beneath the sheet, turning to face the wall. I moved to the desk and turned on the small lamp, tilting it slightly so that the light didn't keep him awake. I tried to read a little of The Philokalia, but I quickly realised how tired I was when I couldn't retain anything or concentrate enough to read things only once. I closed the book and turned off the lamp. The evening sky lit up the window through the curtains, leaving the room in a semi-darkness that was very relaxing. I ran my prayer rope through my fingers and mouthed the Jesus Prayer.

Chapter 10

I slept deeply, and when I woke there was still ten minutes before the alarm was set to go off. I didn't move, but strained to hear the sounds of the Holy Mountain. It was a silence that was distinct, it was filled with God's presence. I got up and stood at the window watching the monastery bathed in moonlight, even the stone of the buildings looked to be resting. But I knew that beyond the silence monks were already beginning their prayer rules, and that the appearance of rest masked the ongoing spiritual labour that was their daily routine.

I dressed and went out into the corridor to find the toilets. The water from the taps was a little warm but felt good as I splashed it into my face. As I returned to our room I looked along to the open archway at the top of the stairs, it was filled with the night sky. I stood in the open air looking at the sea, the moon bore the same markings it always did, the same shadows and craters, but from the Holy Mountain it looked like one of God's servants orbiting the earth. The cloudless sky was full of stars, and I could see beyond their claim to eternity: even in the vast distance of time and space there were limits, time was moving in unimaginable phases, and yet only in the human heart was true eternity to be found in this life. Only when the heart is filled with Christ can man move beyond his mortality.

From my vantage point I could look down on the church and through a small window near the east end I saw the faint glow of a candle. I watched for a moment but couldn't detect any movement, and so headed back to wake Joseph. In fact he was already up and dressed when I returned.

"Did you sleep alright? I asked.

He gave a small grunt, "Why are you up so early?"

"I want to get into church in plenty of time."

"Do you mind if I go a little later, there's no reason to be there ten minutes before the service starts."

"Alright, but make sure you lock the room. I'm going down, I'll see you after the service. Don't forget, we've got permission to receive communion, don't worry about it."

"I wasn't going to, I think you're stressing over nothing." There was a little irritation in his voice and I realised my unnecessary concerns were annoying him.

"Okay Joe, I'll see you down there."

I quietly crept back along the corridor and down the steps into the empty square. I crossed to the church and made the sign of the cross before entering. This time my eyes were already accustomed to the night and I was able to see the icons around me much more clearly. I lit a candle and venerated the saints before moving on through the church. There were around half a dozen monks in their stalls, but as yet no pilgrims. As I venerated Christ, monks began to appear behind me and together we moved across the iconostasis venerating first the Mother of God and then various saints. I felt a little self-conscious moving to the stall I had occupied previously, but no one gave me so much as a glance. Within a few minutes more monks appeared from the shadows and soon all the stalls around me but one were occupied. An elderly Greek priest was shown to the last stall, his beard as long and white as some of the monks.

Two deacons began lighting the candles before the iconostasis and a priest appeared from the royal doors to cense us. As he did so his head remained bowed in a posture of unforced humility. The two groups of singers on opposite sides of the church began to chant their hymns, and once more I found myself being drawn into the reality of prayer. To see men praying who have forsaken the world to seek God is to witness the most profound blend of self-sacrifice and joy. These words of prayer were the core of their lives, the purpose and meaning of every breath that filled their lungs.

I found it easy to dismiss my worldly thoughts and I focussed once more on the icons. The hours began to pass all too quickly, and when I found my mind wandering or distracted, I simply watched the monks performing their liturgical actions and the holy gestures, movements and sounds brought my focus back to God. There were many more monks present than I remembered from my first visit, and the celebration of the Lord's Day added a layer of festivity that brought home the uniqueness of the day. My few words of Greek left me absorbing the intention of the hymns rather than the direct meaning, but I knew enough to recognise when the service moved into the Divine Liturgy. Beyond the royal doors I could see a number of vested priests, and I felt a strong connection with them through my own priesthood.

One of the monks came over to the old Greek priest beside me and gave him a large book. He prodded a place on the page and the priest nodded. When the choir finished singing he began chanting in a soft but clear voice verses in Greek, and my anxiety began to rise. What if I was asked to sing something? How would I explain how little Greek I have? My anxiety rose higher as the same monk then approached me. As the choir sang he bent close to me and said "Father, will you say the Lord's Prayer in English?"

It was initially a huge relief to hear his request, I nodded, "Yes!"

As he walked away, questions began to appear in my head: would they say it in Greek first? Did they want me to sing or intone it? Should I say the whole of the prayer, or only up until "…but deliver us from the evil one" so that the priest in the sanctuary could finish it? As all this began to swirl around my head a tiny doubt appeared – would I even be able to remember the words under these conditions? There is no other prayer I have said as often, we all say it a number of times every day, but suddenly my mind was like a block of concrete.

Inwardly I began running through the words, all the time following the progress of the service to be ready. But the anxiety was groundless, when it came to the moment the monk turned and made a small gesture with his hand and I began to intone the prayer. The familiar rhythm and flow of the words carried me through and all the stress left me. I was even able to focus and pray as I sang. As I ended one of the priests at the altar completed "For Thine is the Kingdom…" in Greek. To participate in a service on Mount Athos, even in this small way, brought me great happiness, and all the stories I had once been told about Athonites being suspicious of English priests were groundless: we were all as Orthodox as one another.

One of the priests appeared at the royal doors and invited us to receive Christ, and some of the monks began queuing to receive. A very young monk came over to me and invited me to enter the sanctuary. As we walked he said "Where abouts are you from Father?" When I told him England, he added "Welcome, it is good to have you with us."

I pushed the door open and walked through a short stone corridor that brought me beside the altar. Around it seven priests were moving as they received Holy Communion. A deacon handed me a golden epitrakhilion which I kissed and placed around my neck. I was invited to wash my hands and then join the line of priests and I watched carefully in case there was some special ceremonial practice that I wasn't aware of. But they received exactly as I was used to doing, and so I bowed my head and slowly moved to the chalice. As I took Christ's Body in my hand I understood that every Divine Liturgy in every church around the world was united to this ritual. I ate slowly, and then moved around the altar once more to drink from the chalice. As Christ's Blood entered me every anxiety, fear or concern was lifted from me. Now that I was united with Christ I felt invulnerable, there was nothing I could do or say that could be a problem.

I was directed to the sink once more, and after returning the vestment I exited through a low arched doorway to the west of the altar. I stepped out into the daylight, to my right a row of monks were sitting along a step on the outside of the church. I walked over to them, unsure what they were doing, and to my surprise the nearest to me was father D.. He got to his feet and grasped my hands. "It is good to see you," he said.

"Have you received communion?" I asked.

"No, we are going in in a moment."

"Why are you out here?"

He smiled, "There's no room in church for us. So many pilgrims."

I could see there was no resentment in his statement, in fact they looked pleased to be sitting out in the sun. "You must come to my room after breakfast," he said, "we must talk."

"Thank you, we would appreciate that."

"You have had communion?"

"Yes," I said.

"We eat food to enable our bodies to roam freely in this world, but we receive Holy Communion that our souls may be free in the next world." He patted my arm, "I will see you later." The monks were going into church and so I followed behind them. As we entered through the main doorway we were met by a crowd of visitors. Sitting at the front I hadn't realised how full the church was behind us, but they parted respectfully to let us through. The monks joined the end of the queue of other monks before the challice, and I went back to my stall. A large plate of antidoron was placed near me on a metal stand, and one of the monks ushered me forwards to take some. As I chewed on it I realised that there would probably never be a moment in my life where I would feel so deeply joyful. After the monks had received communion the pilgrims began to shuffle forwards. As they turned back to return to the places they each came and took some of the bread, while a monk stood close by to supervise if any problems occurred. After a few minutes I saw Joseph approaching the chalice, his head bowed in preparation. Seeing one of my sons receiving Holy Communion on Mount Athos was another special moment, I felt a flood of gratitude for what God had given us.

The service ended with a blessing and the monks began to leave church. I found myself in a group of them and once more the crowd of pilgrims parted to let us through. To my right I saw Joseph, he had been sitting almost directly behind me the whole night, and he smiled as we looked at each other.

Before entering the refectory the monks stood chatting outside, and as the visitors followed us out Joseph came over.

"I heard you saying the Lord's Prayer," he said, still smiling. "I was surprised when you started."

"I met Father D. and he's invited us to his room."

"When, now?"

"No, after breakfast, we need to eat after all that."

"That's great, I really wanted to meet him properly. I'm starving!"

I laughed, and almost on cue, the doors opened and we began to go in.

Chapter 11

We stood behind the benches in the usual way, dishes of food once more laid before us. At the door a large group of monks who had sung in the choir gathered around a book and began to sing. I was unable to discern whether this was because of a particular saint or festival, or if this was their usual practice. Their singing was joyous, it was impossible not to be affected by the spirit of the hymns. When they finished they separated to find places at the tables and the abbot once more blessed the food and us. In unison everyone's hands signed the cross over their chests and we sat to eat. It struck me how much work must have gone into growing and preparing the meal, and I realised I was eating the fruit of the community's labour.

After breakfast both monks and pilgrims gathered in loose groups outside the refectory once more, and I looked around to find Father D.. He was chatting with another monk but then came our way.

"Hello," he said, "we could sit out here in the sun, but I would prefer to drink some tea. Do you want to come to my workshop?"

"That would be lovely, thank you," I said.

He led us down a few steps to a doorway in the corner of the yard, and beyond this was a dark narrow passage to another door. We followed him through into a bright room filled with various tools needed for book binding. In the centre was a long table and he invited us to sit.

"Would you like tea or coffee?"

While he prepared our drinks Joseph and I looked around at the icons on his walls, imagining a life working in such conditions.

Father D. returned without his hat and veil, a soft black cap and waistcoat gave him a far more relaxed appearance. He laid the tray before us and handed Joseph his coffee. "I think you'll like this tea," he said to me, "it is a special blend a visitor makes for me."

He sat at the end of the table, with Joseph and I either side of him. His face was open and friendly, and he seemed to have lost some weight since I last saw him.

"All this equipment is to bind manuscripts and books," he explained, "I get them like this," he reached over and lifted up an unbound wad of pages, "and I turn them into this." He reached over and found a completed book; he clearly took pride in his work.

"Was this your job before coming to Athos?" Joseph asked.

"No, I didn't have a trade before coming, I've learned on the job." He smiled at the thought.

"How did you become a monk?" Joseph asked again.

Father D. turned to face him, he focussed all of his attention on him. "I wasn't a Christian, but I was looking for meaning in life. I had all the fun of the world, parties, drugs, and everyone I knew played music. But there was no real purpose to my life, and I knew there had to be more." As he spoke he didn't turn to look at me, but remained focussed on Joseph. "I began researching different beliefs, I tried everything I could find, and some of it seemed to work for a while, but in the end it didn't last. Then someone I knew suggested I visit Mount Athos. I had heard of it, but didn't really know anything about it. So I accepted the challenge, it seemed an interesting proposal, what did I have to lose? I was in my mid-twenties when I made my first visit. From the moment I arrived I knew I was home."

"Which monastery did you visit?" I asked.

"This one, even on my first visit I knew this was where I was going to live."

"Did you visit any others after that?"

"No, not at that time. Of course I have visited some since, but back then I didn't feel the need to. I left after my first visit a little confused by the experience. What could it mean? How did I make sense of it?"

"How did you make sense of it?" Joseph asked.

"I knew there was a God, a God that we could know. It was an experience I knew was more important than anything else the world could offer. So I went away for a while, I read books, I talked to people, and then I came back. By the end of my second visit I had decided to be a monk." He laughed at his story, as though hearing how it might sound to someone else for the first time.

134

"And since I came to stay I have never wanted to live anywhere else."

"It is a special place," I said, "not just Mount Athos, but the monastery here."

"Yes," he nodded, "and just how special is only something that reveals itself over time. But it is good that you can sense it even as a pilgrim."

"Did you meet Saint Paisios?" Joseph asked.

"Yes, a few times."

"Could you tell he was a saint even when he was alive?" Joseph continued.

"Yes, his holiness was known to the monks here."

"Are there many saints living here?" Joseph persisted.

"There are many saints known only to God, and there are many monks who achieve a profound level of communion with God. But the time of elders like Saint Paisios is over."

I was surprised to hear him say this. "Why do you think that is?" I asked him.

"We are living in difficult days, it is hard for us to be Christian, let alone become saints. We live the monastic life as men have always done, but the heights of spirituality that these great Elders achieved are beyond the reach of modern men."

"Even when you're far from the world?" I said.

"We arrive with the effects of the world in our hearts, we are weak, it is difficult to overcome what modern life does to us. This is an age of self-obsession, where individualism has corrupted the human heart. It is enough to break free of these traps and live a life of repentance. God sees and knows the times we are living in. It has been said that God will reward even the tiniest of faiths at the end because it will be so hard to cling to Him in a world so corrupted."

"Do you think these are the last days?" Joseph said.

"We do not know the exact time, but I do not believe there will be many generations after this one. Saint Paisios told us what must happen before Christ returns, and we are already seeing the beginning of these things."

"What should we look for?" Joseph asked.

"The Jews will rebuild the Temple in Jerusalem, they are already taking control of western life. God blessed them with so much, so many gifts. But like Satan, who, when he fell, corrupted his gifts for the work of evil, so the Jews are using their gifts to achieve worldly power."

I glanced across at Joseph to judge his reaction, but his face was fixed without any flicker of response.

"How should we prepare ourselves? He asked.

Father D. thought for a moment, and then once more his face erupted into a broad smile. "We must prepare just like every generation of Christians has before us. Whatever the future may hold in this world, we each have the assurance that we will die. Whatever the circumstances, and however soon it may come, the devil cannot take our death from us. So we must prepare for judgement, repent and try to sin as little as possible.

Stay faithful to God's commandments and hold on to our faith." He paused for a moment to allow his words to take effect, "It is all as simple as it has ever been. But we try to complicate things because our ego doesn't want to accept that this could be it. We crave special secrets, go looking for esoteric teachings. No, we don't need any of it. Christianity is really simple. We must go to church, receive Holy Communion, say our prayers and try to treat other people as well as we can. We can only do this if we hold on to hope, hope in Christ's promises. If we see ourselves from a worldly perspective we will go mad. Just look at the world, it has lost its mind. People are suffering depression, there is suicide, abortion, families are falling apart: anyone can see that the materialism of the humanists has failed. Liberal culture has no answers, it only sets people loose into an illusion of freedom, but in fact it enslaves people. It is a madness that no one is immune to, not even in the Church."

"How do you see it affecting the Church?" I said.

"We have priests visit us who are at their wits end. They try to hold fast to Orthodoxy but there are bishops telling them to accept worldly thinking. I know of a number of priests who have been forced out of their posts because they will not accept ecumenism. But this is only to be expected, Christ warned us that in the end the Church will be small, but it will not disappear. At the very end the Church will be found in caves and mountains, Christians will take to the catacombs because they won't be tolerated by the world anymore."

"What about the monks on Athos?" I said. "Will life here continue as it is?"

"I don't know is the honest answer. I pray that it will. I know there are monks who believe it will be the last place on earth to hold out to Antichrist. Saint Paisios said there would be a time of great growth in Orthodoxy before the end. That after the war many will turn to God again, and the heretics will renounce their falsehood. Saint Porphyrius believed this too. If you go up to the peak of Mount Athos, there is a monk nearly at the top single handedly building a monastery." His smile widened once more.

"Is he doing this because he thinks many more men will become monks?" I said.

"Partly, but mainly because it was one of the last instructions Saint Porphyrius gave to him before he died. The disciple continues to be obedient to his elder, and the monastery is being built."

I marvelled at such faith, here we were immersed in a world where worldly conventions about good sense and wisdom were irrelevant. I was aware that time was moving on, and I wanted to take the opportunity to ask about prayer. "Father, can you say something about the Jesus Prayer?"

"You are already saying it I presume?" He said.

"Yes, but is there anything you can say that might help."

His face became more focussed, "Do you use the prayer spontaneously, or are you following a rule?"

"I don't have a rule, but I try to use my rope every day. I do say it spontaneously as well, depending on where I am or what I'm doing." As I said it I realised how undisciplined it sounded, and even revealing it to a monk on Athos was enough to make me resolve to better structure how I said it.

"What is most important is how we approach the Jesus Prayer," he explained. "Some of the Saints call it watchfulness, or sobriety of the heart, but it all amounts to the same thing: inner silence. If we have no attention to the words we say then how can there be real repentance? The heart and mind must be focussed, to the exclusion of all else. Saint Macarios says the heart must become so full of love for God that we become blind to the material world: the heart filled with love sees only God. Few of us will ever achieve this level of prayer, but the principle is the same. When we have attention we do not doubt God's mercy, we genuinely repent, believing in God's love for us. Faith born in this kind of attention has no desire for anything more, the heart is filled with a longing for God that disperses all other desires and thoughts. In his wisdom Saint Paul sets before us the three great pillars of faith, hope and love. This order isn't arbitrary, each is the garden in which the next grows. When we say the Jesus Prayer with attention, faith grows within us. From this kind of faith sprouts hope, because we focus on our sins, but also on the eternal mercy of God. All true Christian hope has at its centre this one great truth, that God is merciful. When this hope is born us, love for God is nurtured because the heart responds to its merciful maker, we begin to understand beyond words how we are cherished by God, and so we love in return. If this love is genuine, it will pour out for all of God's creation, but especially for our fellow man. Attention enables us to understand ourselves created in God's image, not just ourselves as individuals, but all humanity. Recognising God's image in one another, the image of the One we love, we cannot but love everyone." Sensing that he was saying a lot at once he paused again, and quietly waited for our thoughts to assemble. He continued, "These are lofty words, but we must do the simple thing. When we say the Jesus Prayer we must avoid being distracted, we must focus carefully on the words we are saying, allow the true meaning to penetrate our minds. We mustn't rush the prayer, it is better to say it two or three times properly than rush thoughtlessly through it a hundred times. When the mind is absorbed with the meaning, if we have tried to repent of our sins, if we have been faithful to God, then the Holy Spirit may permit the prayer to move from our mind to our heart. This may come and go, there are few who live continuously in this condition, but God may permit us times when the heart is awakened in prayer. But it is also important to see that the prayer is linked to the whole of our life. Saying the Jesus Prayer isn't an isolated activity in one small corner of our lives. It is dependent on the way we are living. If we live as a tree which grows only for God, then the fruit of the prayer will be full of life. But the fruit cannot grow by itself, it needs the whole tree. The Jesus prayer isn't a magic spell or incantation, but it is full of power. Even if the prayer doesn't move beyond the lips, it is like a burning fire to the demons. They flee from us when we seek God through the prayer, but when we are negligent they make their home with us. This can be seen in modern life where fewer people pray than ever before. Church attendance is in decline, people don't take their spiritual state seriously. The demons barely need to do the work anymore, because people freely give themselves to vice and idolatry. Not that they know this, so many are ignorant to the truth and have begun to see evil as good, just as we were told they would. The time is coming soon when Christianity will be considered an evil. Christians will be rejected as judgemental, unloving, because they have stayed true to God's laws. As these things develop, we will need to pray more than ever before."

"Is it possible to pray properly while living in the world?" Joseph asked.

"Prayer is not a technique, or a system," Father D. said softly, "but it can be taught. The tradition of monasticism is that we learn the path of prayer with the guidance of an experienced traveller. There are many pitfalls along this path, many ways we can become deceived. We may think we are following the path when really the demons are leading us to damnation. So it is necessary to have someone to ask advice, someone we trust in these matters. But as I said, today we are so weak that visions and great spiritual gifts should never be desired. If we chase these things we will become the plaything of the demons. Instead we must do what we can, say our prayers regularly and focus on living a Christian life as best we can. We must listen to our conscience, let it develop so that we hear it clearly. If we ignore the voice of our conscience it gets quieter and quieter until we can't hear it at all. This is how we must live in the world, keep it simple."

"Please can you explain why some monks use breathing exercises when they say the prayer?" I said.

"This is not something anyone should attempt without clear spiritual guidance. It can lead quickly to problems."

"Yes, I have said that to people myself," I assured him. "But can you explain how we can distinguish between techniques and systems from what monks are doing when they use breathing exercises."

"I would not call them exercises. We must first understand what is going on. True prayer meets with Christ in the heart. Our Lord makes His dwelling place here," he patted his chest, "if we make it a suitable dwelling place for Him. The heart is surrounded by the lungs, and when hesychasts follow their breath they are focussing on the channel that leads to the heart. Their attention is drawn in with the breath to that place where Christ dwells, but it isn't like Buddhist mediation where tricks are used to affect the brain. Does that make sense to you?"

"Yes, thank you Father," I nodded, "and how does this help the saints?"

"It helps because the more we guide our attention to dwell with Christ within us, the less we are inclined to allow our attention to go wandering off. When the mind discovers the sweetness of Christ, why would it want what the world has to offer? The more time we spend in the heart, the more natural it becomes, until even when we are sleeping or working, the sweetness of Christ's presence sustains us. When we read about many martyrs, they have known this sweetness even as their physical bodies were violated. It is greater than any physical sensation or experience."

"Do the saints stop saying the Jesus Prayer when they reach this state?" Joseph asked.

"No," said Father D., "it is vital that we continue to say the prayer even if the mind should become permanently fixed in the heart. Because even then we may become deluded or confused by dreams and fantasies. The imagination is a powerful part of the mind, but it is on the edges of the mind, it isn't at the core. The demons do not know our inner, deepest thoughts, but they can prompt images at the periphery of our mind. By continuing to say the Jesus Prayer we protect the mind from this kind of attack. The demons never give up in trying to catch us out. Look at this." He stood up and fetched an icon from a shelf. It was of the Ladder of Divine Ascent.

"We have a print of that icon in our house," said Joseph.

"The Ladder described by Saint John is a warning to us," said Father D.. He pointed to the monks being pulled from near the top of the ladder. "Do you see these here, they nearly made it. They climbed higher than most men could ever imagine. But even so high the demons pull them to the abys. We must never let our guard down, pride and ego never leave us. We must persist in our struggles until we die."

"Why does God permit this when men have learned the habit of prayer?" Joseph said. I immediately remembered what Father I. had said, and was relieved when Father D. echoed his words.

"Prayer is not a habit. The different virtues may become a habit if we repeat them often enough. It is easy to learn the habit of being kind or generous to our neighbour. But prayer is different. The corrupted, old man within us forever resists prayer. Of all that we can do, prayer is the one thing the demons hate most. They will do anything to prevent us from praying. Think of those nagging thoughts that suggest reasons why we shouldn't attend church or stand before our icons at home. This continues until the moment of our death. Prayer is a struggle the whole of our life because our struggle is with our enemy. The Psalmist says we must smash the heads of the babies of our enemies. He is talking about these thoughts born of the demons. So, to answer your question, no man ever learns prayer as a habit, but we can learn it through constant struggle. And God desires this effort because it is like fire to a steel blade. When

144

we are tested, when we must pray through sheer force of will, the Fathers say there is no higher prayer, no prayer more acceptable to God. It is as valuable as shedding our blood for Christ, when we force ourselves to pray it is a spiritual martyrdom."

"One last question Father," Joseph continued, "how do we drive away unwanted thoughts?"

Fr D. nodded again, "This is a question that many people ask. Unwanted thoughts are something ancient, there is nothing new about it. Monks with many years of experience have battled against logismoi, because part of our struggle is this control of the mind that I have been describing. Our thoughts skip this way and that, if we allow them to dance without restraint the demons can prompt all kinds of images into our heads. It is so easy to be led away from Christ in this way." He paused and looked carefully at Joseph's face, as though studying his response. "As beginners in prayer we cannot expect to master them by ourselves, we must rely entirely on God to rid us of them. It takes great spiritual strength to control the mind, but even the spiritually strong are dependent on God. Unwanted thoughts feed on cold hearts, and so we must warm them up. Do you understand what I mean by this?"

"I'm not sure," admitted Joseph, "could you explain?"

"The heart is warmed by prayer, when we say Christ's name with our heart it brings us spiritual warmth. Though there are some who describe a physical sensation of this warming too, the physical organ is warmed. When we call on Christ he comes with power, he is like a fire that burns the demons, he scatters unwanted thoughts. It is God Who protects us, this is spiritual strength, it is not anything we create or achieve in that sense."

"Saying the Jesus Prayer," Joseph said softly.

"Yes, but sometimes even this needs help. If we are sitting in a chair, it can be good to stand up and raise our arms to God, or make a prostration before an icon. These physical acts help us. We are comprised of body and soul, not two separate things, but one whole person. When we perform sacred actions they affect the soul. This is why we must not be too casual, not just about prayer but in everything we do. When we work, or study, we must approach all things with a certain seriousness, sobriety, because everything we do is helping to form us. In this way we can turn our whole life into an offering to God, even jobs we don't want to do. Nothing should be seen as a waste of time, because with the right spirit we can make every moment count. We who are not perfect must struggle until our death, but there are saints who have conquered unwanted thoughts."

"Can you recommend someone I should read on this?" Joseph asked.

"Yes, look up Saint Gregory of Sinai, there is a lot of help in his writings."

"I will, thank you."

I looked at the clock, "We've taken a lot of your time. Thank you for being so generous with us."

"It is a joy to have you here. I feel I have been visited by angels." Father D. said this without any hint of humour, and I was a little embarrassed at his kindness. We stood up, and Father D. held out his hands and asked for a blessing. The realisation that the priesthood was not dependent on my own worth was vivid at such moments, and I gave him a blessing. As we walked towards the door there was a knock. Father D. stepped past us and opened it to find two young pilgrims standing in the hall.

"Are we early?" One of them asked, seeing us there.

"Not at all, please come in," said Father D.

Joseph and I thanked him again and followed the passage out into the bright square. "We need to ask the guest master what time the ferry is due, "I said.

"Okay, I've still got the key to the room," said Joseph, "I'll see you back there."

I knocked at the door and heard movement inside the room. The friendly face of the guest master appeared, "Hello," he said in his Greek accent.

"Father, can you tell me the time of the ferry to Daphne?"

"Yes, you have just over an hour."

"Thank you," I said, "and thank you for letting us stay."

"Has your pilgrimage been going well?"

"Yes, full of blessings."

"It is important for priests in the world to take time to visit monasteries, otherwise they might lose the vision of what the priesthood means."

"Do you get many priests from other countries?"

"Yes," he said, "from all over the world."

"Have you been on Athos a long time?"

"Seventeen years, I should have come sooner," he laughed. "But all things in God's time."

Joseph was packing his bag as I entered, "That was more than I expected," he said.

"It's more than his words isn't it?"

"Yea, I need time to reflect on all that. How long have we got?"

"About an hour," I said, "we can take our bags and sit by the sea if you want."

We tidied what little disturbance our stay had had on the room and carried our bags down into the Monastery square. "I need to leave some money," I said.

"Who will you give it to? The guest master?"

"No, I'll stick it in one of the collection boxes inside the church."

Joseph sat on one of the benches while I went back into the now empty church. The air was still thick with the sweet smell of incense, and the icons looked like they were waiting for the monks to return. I pushed some money into a slot in the wall, and lit a final candle. I pushed it into the metal holder before the icon of the Archangel Michael and asked him to pray for us. Outside Joseph looked relaxed, he stood as I approached and pulled his bag onto his back. I looked around at the buildings one last time, every brick seemed to have been shaped in paradise, and as an old monk walked across the courtyard we left through the arched gateway towards the dock.

Descending the steep slope down to the sea we looked out over the few monastery buildings and watched a young monk with a long ginger beard hanging out sheets in front of his balcony. He was a picture of contentment, and I envied his peace. Next to where the ferries docked was a shaded area with seat. I dropped my bag and turned one of the wooden seats so I could look out at the sea.

"I'm going to walk up to the end of the bay," said Joseph, "we've got plenty of time."

I watched as he wandered off into the distance, and then felt a little concern when he began climbing the rocks there. If we had been anywhere else I would have shouted for him to be careful, but in the quiet of the monastery I could only look on with unease. He disappeared from view, and I began to worry even more. But a few minutes later he emerged from the rock next to the beach and began to walk back towards me. About half way along the bay he stooped to stroke a cat which had trotted towards him, and I couldn't resist taking another photograph.

As Joseph climbed the steps to where I was sitting a large group of pilgrims appeared behind me, chatting enthusiastically in Greek. They had timed it perfectly, because within a minute the blue and white ferry chugged its way around the coastline, the signal for us all to head for the dock.

Chapter 12

The gate lowered at the bow of the ferry as it approached the dock. The group of Greek men stepped back when they realised that they were directly in its path, but the grinding of its contact with the stone wall was the signal for us to step aboard. A proper ticket desk wasn't needed with so few of us being picked up, and one of the crew stood ready to take our coins and hand out tickets. We purchased a trip to Daphne, with the intention of walking the hour to our next monastery. I wasn't sure if the regular bus service would be available on a Sunday, but we were both eager to make the short walk. As the ferry began to reverse from the shore, it started to rock again, but having survived it once, we were less anxious now that we assumed it was normal. We climbed to the upper deck but there were no spare seats and every available place at the rails was taken. So instead we went back down to the lower deck and leaned against the rail at the stern. As we pulled away from the shore we had an incredible view of the peak of Mount Athos, and on a hot day the streaks of ice that marked it made us realise how high it must be.

"Hard to imagine that monk up there by himself building the monastery," I said.

"I can't see any sign of him from down here."

"It must be a task just to get the material up there, let alone the building equipment."

"Yea," said Joseph, "but I don't think difficulty stops them being obedient. In fact it probably adds to the sense of it."

As we watched the coast passing in reverse from our last trip, we fell silent, content to think through the events of our visit so far. Being on the ferry brought home to me the fleeting nature of our experience with the monks, and how permanent things were for them. I envied the peace and security of their lives, but I knew I didn't have a monastic calling. For one thing, my son was standing beside me, and my other son waited for us at home with his mother. God had blessed me with the joys and demands of family life, and this was the setting for my own journey to God. I knew I had to take what I could from these visits, but I had no secret desire to join them. For one thing, in my heart I knew I wasn't up to it. It was a life that was beyond my emotional and psychological capacities, I needed the support and closeness of my wife. I looked at Joseph and began to wonder where God would lead him. At this I began to pray for him, even as I gazed at the Holy Mountain.

We were joined by three men speaking in Romanian, they looked to be in their early thirties, they pointed at things they spotted, and their conversation was full of excitement. The one nearest to us turned to me and asked "Which monastery have you been to?" His English was very good.

"Gregoriou, what about you?"

"We have been at St. Paul's for three days, but now we are going home."

"Three days! I thought you could only stay for a single night at each monastery," I said with surprise.

"Yes, but we have friends here," he smiled, "they break the rules a little for us. We come very year."

"Are you from Romania?"

"Yes, how did you know?"

"We have some Romanians in our parish in England. Ear must be getting tuned to it "

"It is very sad, many young people are leaving Romania; the country is in a terrible mess." His friends said something to him in Romanian, and he confirmed to them what he had said.

"Is it just the economic situation?" I asked.

"It is a mixture of different things, but yes, mainly the economics. The population is a fraction of what it should be because everyone is forced to look for work elsewhere. And as a result there are not enough taxes being paid, so the government doesn't have enough to pay for good healthcare, or all the usual things that need to be done. We are lucky," he gestured at his friends with his thumb, "we have work and are paid well. We work for a Russian company that has spent money in our town, and as long as they stay we will too."

"Is it the effects of Communism that has left Romania like this?"

"Strangely, no. I am no friend of Communism, I know of a priest who was taken away and never seen again. This is true, in the final years they were still disappearing people. But the press didn't mention it, and I wonder how many times it happened across the country without anyone outside of their parishes ever finding out. But one thing the Communists did was ensure that there was work for everyone. If a man was walking down the street during the day, they would stop him and ask him why he wasn't in work. If he had no reason, they would take him and force him to take a job. But now there are no jobs to find and everyone is on the take."

"You mean the government? " I said.

"Yes, the government, but ordinary people too. God forgive me for saying this, but there are people in the Church too that only think of money. Everyone is looking for a way to make cash, and so no one trusts anyone. When there are jobs available, even for the government, you must pay up front to get it."

"Corruption," I said.

"Yes, corruption, it breaks my heart to see our country this way."

"But I've seen articles describing churches and monasteries being built all over Romania, it looks like the Church is flourishing."

"It is true, we are free to be Orthodox again without fear, but even this is a chance for some to make money. When a new church is to be built, the companies will charge double for their work, they over charge for everything, so that even the Church is robbed."

I stood, shaking my head, unsure how to respond. "The Romanians I've met in England are all good people. "

"Please don't misunderstand me, most Romanians are faithful people. But like anywhere, it is the minority that is in charge, the minority who ruin life for everyone else. But Romania is a beautiful country, there are many holy shrines, and as you say, many monasteries to visit. We live just outside of our town and it is beautiful. Have you ever been to Romania?"

"No, but every time I see footage I think about it."

He pulled out a notepad, "Please, I will give you my address, and my contact numbers. When you want to come to Romania, call me. I will arrange everything. I have contacts in the monasteries, and you can stay with members of my family. Would you like to come?"

I was surprised at the offer, "That is very kind of you, thank you. Let me give you my contact details too." I wrote my email address into his note book, and he studied what I had written.

"Father Spyridon? Saint Spyridon is a great saint, you know how he stopped the Roman Catholics building a church near his relics?"

"Yes," I grinned, "I am blessed to be named after him."

"Where are you going next?" He asked.

"I can't pronounce the name of the monastery, it begins with an X. The one next to Daphne." I rummaged around in the top of my bag, trying to find the sheet of paper with the details.

"Xiropotamou?" He said.

"I'm not sure, I've got it written down. Is that one between Daphne and Panteleimon?"

"Yes," he said, "I have never been there."

I found the sheet and ran my finger down the list of our schedule, but instead of "Xiropotamou" it said "Xenofonta". I stared at it for a moment, wondering if I had written it out incorrectly. I showed him the paper, "I've written this," I said stupidly.

He shook his head vigorously, "No, this is further along the peninsula."

I turned in horror, "Joe, I've messed up the booking."

"What's happened?"

"You know I can never pronounce the name of our next monastery, well I've booked us in to another one beginning with X." He frowned and stared back at me. "Will the ferry drop us off there?"

The Romanian man dismissed the idea, "No, on a Sunday the ferry calls at Daphne and then goes straight to Ouranoupolis."

"How far is it to walk?" Joseph asked.

"Too far to walk," he said, "but you might be able to get one of the taxis."

"A taxi will drive us all the way?" I said.

"No, no, a taxi boat. There is a booking office in the restaurant at Ouranoupolis. You can hire a ride

155

along the coast. I don't think they are very expensive."

A wave of relief flooded through me, "We'll do that Joe."

Joseph smiled, "Sounds good."

"Good luck," said the Romanian man, "and come and visit us."

"Thank you, and thank you for helping us."

He laughed, "God is taking care of you."

My pride was dented, I had made a big show of being in control and organising our trip, even to the point of getting bus time tables for Thessalonica. This had partly been to assure my wife that our son was going to be safe with me, but now I would have to explain what I'd done. If I had made the effort to speak the name of the monastery out loud I would have spotted the mistake, but seeing a word beginning with X I had jumped to the conclusion it was the one I wanted. I decided that no matter how much the taxi boat would cost, it was worth paying, and we could catch the ferry for the final stretch of the journey when we had to leave. I relaxed, the looming disaster seemed to have been averted.

As the ferry approached Daphne we couldn't see many people waiting, but as we drew to the shore a door opened in a low building to our right and a crowd of pilgrims spilled out towards us. I remembered from my first visit that this was the custom house where particular pilgrims would have their bags checked if it was believed something had been stolen from Athos. As the bow lowered, there was only one monk alighting with us, and Daphne ahead of us looked deserted. It reminded me of Sunday afternoons from my childhood when shops were always closed and there was this same sense of pause before the rest of the week began. As soon as we were off the ticket seller began dealing with the huge crowd of men before him.

We walked briskly to the restaurant, and leaving my bag outside with Joseph I went in to find out about the taxis. At the far end of the room was a table with a cardboard sign beside it listing the prices of the taxis. But there was no one manning it, so I went over to the till. "Who do I speak to about booking a taxi boat?"

"No, not today." His face didn't change expression as he delivered the news, "they run again tomorrow."

"Are there any buses or other transport going along the coast towards Ouranoupolis?"

"No, not until tomorrow."

"What time is the next ferry?"

He pointed out through the door, "That is the last one."

I rushed outside and explained the situation to joseph.

"What shall we do?" He said.

"We can't stay here, and it's too far to walk. We could turn up at the other monastery and hope for the best, like them French blokes did, but it's taking a risk."

"What do you think we should do?"

I looked at the last couple of pilgrims waiting to board the ferry, "We need to get back on."

We grabbed our bags and ran back to the dock, as we arrived all the passengers had boarded and they were preparing to raise the bow. The crewman could see we hadn't come through the customs house and he looked suspicious.

I pulled out our tickets, "We just got off by accident," I blurted, "we should have stayed on."

Without asking for further payment he waved us to go past him as the chains began rolling back into the ship. The ferry was now even more crowded, but it was a relief to be back on board. We found a wall to lean against and catch our breath. "Are you disappointed not to be visiting another monastery?" I asked.

"Not at all. It would have been good to see another one, but we can have an extra day in Thessalonica now. We can visit Saint Paisios." I was relieved at his reaction, he seemed genuinely happy at the change of plan.

The ferry headed further out from the shore and without the usual stops at the monasteries, made good time. It was good to see Panteleimon monastery once more, but as we passed the little monastery of Xenofonta I realised I had no way of contacting the monks to apologise for our failure to turn up. I thought about the priest's flat in Thessalonica, and as long as no one else was staying there that night, at least we wouldn't be faced with any additional cost. The sudden rush and change of plans left me agitated, and so I focussed on the physical terrain of the peninsula and took some photographs of the passing monasteries in the hope of distracting myself.

The square tower in Ouranoupolis came into sight and the ferry pulled closer to the shoreline. Above the beaches were luxury hotels, and after being with the monks it was strange to see crowds of people in their swimwear frolicking on the sand. Bikini-clad women were lying in the sun, and the sight of so much naked flesh was unwelcome.

"Do we have time to get something to eat before the bus leaves?" Joseph asked.

"I should think so, and if we're rushed we can grab something to eat on the way."

A few wives stood at the dock to greet their returning men, and as the pilgrims walked back into town, surrounded by bars and restaurants, we knew we had returned to the world. Joseph and I decided to check that the bus times corresponded to the details I had taken from the internet before we went searching for food. But as we climbed the slight incline up from the dock two young Greek men called out from behind us. "Father! Hello Father."

We turned to find the two men who had knocked at Father D.'s door as we had been leaving. "Hello," I said, "I recognise you from Gregoriou."

"Are you going to Thessalonica?" The taller of the two men asked.

"Yes," I said, anticipating that some bad news about the buses was about to be shared with us.

"We have a car, would you like a lift?"

Chapter 13

"My name is Dimitri," he said as he lifted open the boot of his car. "This is Kostas." He unstrapped two booster seats for young children from the car's rear seat and tossed them into the boot. Amongst his bags and tools were two plastic light sabres.

"Your children like Star Wars?" I said.

"Yes," he admitted sheepishly, perhaps thinking we might judge him for it.

"My boys were the same when they were younger," I assured him.

He lifted our bags into the boot and invited me to sit in the passenger seat beside him. As soon as the doors clunked shut he switched on the air conditioning, the first time I had been in a car with such luxury, and I was very grateful for it.

"Where abouts do you live?" I asked

"In Thessaloniki," he said, turning to see if there was any traffic. He pulled out onto the empty road and I remembered the Romanian man's observation that God was looking after us.

"Do you think you'll stay there long term?"

"It is hard to say," said Dimitri, "as long as work doesn't dry up we have no reason to leave. We both work in telecommunications, there is plenty of business for us at the moment. But many of our friends have gone."

"Do you mean they've left Thessalonica, or Greece?"

"Greece," he said, "the economy is in such bad shape. They had no choice." Hearing him echo the description of conditions in Romania made me wonder how things across the EU could be going so badly.

"Who do you think is to blame?" I said.

"Of course, it is the banks. Everyone in Greece knows this. The German banks are stripping our country of all its assets, the factories, airports, businesses, they do not pay a fair price and now we must pay them for services which once belonged to Greece."

"Do you see any way out of it?" I said.

"No, things are only getting worse. I don't know where it is going to lead."

From behind me Kostas added "Yes, Dimitri, but let's be honest, we got ourselves in a mess even before the Germans came."

"Yes, this is true," said Dimitri, "no one wanted to pay their taxes, especially the rich. But what has happened is the rich continue to get richer, while the poor are paying for their dishonesty. There are plenty of nice apartments still being built, but many people cannot even feed their families. And the government can do nothing. The EU and the bankers have forced them to sign papers promising not to spend anything on welfare or the things that ordinary people need. It is a disgrace."

Kostas added "We are doing everything we can to destroy our beautiful country." There was a genuine sadness in his voice, it seemed out of place coming from such a young man.

"How is this affecting people's faith?" I said.

"It is a difficult subject Father," said Dimitri, "I do not want to judge people. But Greek culture is struggling to stay alive. American influences have brought so many negative things, people's ideas about life are changing. Many young people only want to have fun, they do not consider the important things."

"I think that's probably true everywhere," I assured him, "and true of most of us before we grow up a little."

"Yes Father," said Dimitri, "I am not claiming to be good. But even in my short life I can see a difference. Young girls have no shame anymore, they walk down the street half naked, they stick pins in their faces; they have forgotten what life is."

"They see all this on the television and they think it's normal," said Kostas. "I don't think it is an accident."

"What do you mean?" I asked him.

"I believe there is a deliberate attempt to destroy Greek culture." He paused, and then corrected himself. "No, not just Greek culture, but Orthodox culture. I am not claiming that Greece was a perfect example of how Orthodox people should live, but at least there was faith. Today the schools are teaching all kinds of nonsense, and what was a shared faith in our culture is being side-lined. It is happening very suddenly, and is embraced by advertisers and big companies. But then, the saints warned us that such things would come. But still it is upsetting to see."

We fell into silence and looked out at the hills as we snaked our way to Thessalonica. It struck me how little farming there seemed to be, and how much of the landscape was left to itself. So much of it looked parched and inhospitable, and I secretly thought it didn't look so beautiful. I noticed how many half-built houses there were along the road, many of which looked abandoned, a physical sign of the country's economic woes. I began to think about the next couple of days, and asked "How far is it from Thessalonica to the monastery where Saint Paisios is buried?"

"The Monastery of Saint John the Theologian? About twenty minutes by taxi," said Dimitri, "it is a beautiful place, but there are sometimes hundreds of pilgrims, you need to get there early in the morning to miss the crowds."

"We should go tomorrow," said Joseph.

"We'll have a look at the map," I said, "it might be best to go when we're closer to the airport."

Signs for Thessalonica began promising we were only fifteen miles from our destination. "Will you be able to drop us off near the bus station?" I asked.

"Is that where you are staying?" Dimitri asked.

"No, I thought we could get a bus from there."

"I will drive you to your door, what is the address?"

I rummaged around in my pocket and pulled out a crumpled slip of paper. I read the address aloud, and Dimitri confirmed with Kostas where it was. "That's on our way, I know that area."

As we entered the outskirts of Thessalonica we saw a large group of riot police standing at the side of the road. "What's happening? " I said.

"There are strikes today," said Kostas, "the strikers are marching and threatening to close off some of the streets. But it won't affect our route."

"Wages have been frozen for a long time," added Dimitri, "people cannot deal with their living standards going down any further."

He turned off the wide duel-carriageway onto a very narrow side street. The five-storey buildings on either side looked straight out of Communist-era Moscow, only their balconies broke up the harsh, repetitive shapes: they looked cheap and as though they had been built in a hurry. "This part of Thessaloniki was burned in a fire," said Kostas, as though he was reading my thoughts. "When you visit the other half of the city you will see a better side." There were parked cars on both sides of the street, some left jutting out at ridiculous angles, leaving just a single car's width between them. Each time we met an oncoming vehicle Dimitri would stop and negotiate with the other driver who would reverse. As I looked out I couldn't help thinking it was one of the ugliest places I had ever visited. The graffiti only added to the impression, and I wondered if my reaction was because I had just come from the idyll of Mount Athos.

Dimitri counted the building numbers as he drove, until he found a space outside one just five numbers down from our apartment. He pulled over, and immediately the doors were opened a wall of heat rushed in and hit us in the face. As Dimitri lifted our bags from the car Kostas climbed out to say goodbye. We expressed our thanks for their kindness, and both men asked for a blessing, "If you go to see Saint Paisios, please pray for my family," said Dimitri. I promised I would, and still waving they drove away.

"That was incredible," said Joseph, "right to the door."

"And the money we saved on bus fare we can spend on food for the extra day in town."

As we wandered along the pavement looking for our number we passed a pub called "The Dirty Duck". The sign was in English, and though it was shut and the lights were out, inside I could see the shirts of various English football clubs hanging on the walls.

"Look Joe," I said pointing to a smaller sign, "free Wi-Fi. We'll have to come here later and send a message to your mom."

Our building had a large glass front with the number painted across it. I tried the key we had borrowed and to our relief the door swung open and we entered the shaded foyer. Our apartment was on the top floor and we decided to take the lift. As the doors slid open we found ourselves looking at a tiny space that would barely take two men, let alone their luggage.

"You go up with the bags," said Joseph, "I'll take the stairs.

The interior of the lift was entirely covered in mirrors, and as it carried me up I stood looking at the sunburned bearded face looking back at me; I chuckled at how comical I looked. The doors opened and I walked along a dark corridor to our flat, and as I fumbled with the keys I heard the sound of Joseph trotting up the stairs. A fire-door swung open and he looked around to find me. I had the key in the lock, and by the time he caught up with me I was stepping into the apartment.

It consisted of one bedroom, a kitchen, a living room and a shower room. Three of the rooms had metal shutters pulled across large glass doorways, and as I unlocked the one in the kitchen I discovered a balcony that ran the entire length of the apartment. I stepped out into the sunshine and looked down at the street below. A young couple were arguing in Greek, and for a moment I watched with amusement as the brow-beaten young man was chastised by his girlfriend. They wandered off and I studied the apartments opposite. There was no sign of life anywhere, not even any washing on the lines. We were a long way up, and I tried to imagine how a fire engine could force its way through the congested narrow street, and in the end decided it was best not to give it too much thought if I was going to sleep peacefully.

The apartment belonged to a Greek priest who worked in Athens: this was his holiday flat. The décor gave the impression of a cultured, elderly man, and feeling grubby and in need of a shower I felt a little out of place. Joseph was unpacking in the bedroom, he had the shutters pulled open and a breeze was billowing the curtains across the bed.

"The sofa isn't big enough to sleep on," he observed.

"It's a big bed, can you bare to share it with your dad?"

"No problem."

I showered and found Joseph watching television. He was flicking channels, trying to find something in English. "While you're in the shower, I'm going to visit the pub, I need to send an email to the monastery to explain why we didn't turn up."

"What about Saint Paisius?" Joseph asked.

"When we've got internet connection we can find it on a map. We can make a decision then."

Joseph nodded, but I secretly doubted we would have time.

The Dirty Duck was open when I arrived with my Kindle. I was the only customer, and the very young barmaid came straight to me. I ordered a beer and asked for the password for their Wi Fi which she gave to me on a business card which had the pub sign printed on the reverse. I sent my apologies to the monastery and emailed my other son to let him know how things were going. Just then a man entered and sat at the bar, I noticed the barmaid say something to him and they looked my way. I had come out without my rassa, hoping to avoid attention. He called across to me, "You are from England?"

"Yes," I smiled, "I like your pub."

The walls were decorated with a bizarre mixture of English paraphernalia, not just football shirts, but music posters from the 1970s advertising tours by bands like Jethro Tull, and a signed poster of George Best.

"It was my sister's idea," he explained, "we opened before the recession. She lived in London for a year and wanted to open an English pub. But people don't come out in the evening any more, it is not a good time for business. Do you live near Manchester?"

"No, I'm from the Midlands."

"Mid-lands," he repeated slowly, "which teams come from there?"

I listed a few local premiership and ex-premiership teams but the only one he recognised was Aston Villa. As we chatted Joseph appeared and I noticed the barmaid glance his way. We bought a round of drinks and the barmaid brought over a complimentary bowl of crisps (or chips as they call them).

"Have you had a look at the map?" Joseph said.

"No, hang on," I opened up my device again and we searched for maps of Thessalonica. But we weren't sure of the village, and had to look for St. Paisios' grave. The village of Souroti looked to be close to the airport, and we agreed to leave it a day, and visit on the way to our final hotel. This gave us a whole day free to tour the churches of Thessalonica, and the owner of the pub was keen to give us directions. It turned out that amongst the strikers were the bus drivers, but he assured us that we were only a twenty minute walk from the city sites. The beer relaxed us and we ended up staying for a meal. By the time we headed back to the apartment we had a couple more drinks and were feeling properly reunited with the world. We spent a while flicking through Greek television until we landed on the E Channel, which was broadcasting a church service. After a while Joseph headed to bed, but I sat watching, trying to figure out what was going on, much to his amusement: "Better than Songs Of Praise!" I shouted after him.

I watched the priest intoning the office, and my thoughts returned to the monks on the Holy Mountain. I became aware of the effect of the alcohol and the large meal we had eaten, and I regretted rushing into the pleasures of worldly life. I leaned my head back on the sofa and let the memories of the past few days bring their images before me. In the rush of the day we hadn't paused to pray, and I felt its absence.

Chapter 14

We woke early and I went out for some bread and meat. At a local corner shop I found a small map of the city which gave the impression that everything was simple to find. Joseph was drinking coffee on the balcony when I returned and I passed him the map.

"The churches are marked on it," I said, "we should be able to walk everywhere."

"And we'll visit Saint Paisios tomorrow?"

"Yes," I assured him, "don't worry."

The streets were busy with traffic as we walked to the other side of Thessalonica, it took around twenty minutes to reach the area that had survived the fire, and it created a very different impression to the modern half of the city. Instead of the cheap looking structures we found ourselves surrounded by spacious streets of white stone buildings, and everything was laid out in a simple grid that made it easy even for the first time visitor to find their way around. We wanted to see as much as we could, but our priority was to visit the churches of Saint Demetrius and Hagia Sophia. We crossed the busy duel carriageways and managed to avoid the swarms of scooters that gathered at every set of traffic lights. I was struck by how many young people there were around, and despite the accounts of economic collapse, the busyness of the city gave the impression that it was thriving.

Our first target was the church of Saint Demetrius, we had been told repeatedly by friends that we must visit, and as we approached we understood why. It is a huge building which was originally built in the fifth century, and its great age is immediately apparent. As we entered the impact was of icons and huge golden chandeliers. The icons were darkened with age, and gave a sense of sobriety. We joined a small queue and venerated a large icon of Saint Demetrius astride his horse. We lit our candles and walked through the church towards the iconostasis. Above us shafts of light penetrated the shadows, illuminating the mosaics that decorated every wall. Rows of empty wooden chairs filled the nave and we sat a few rows from the front to take in the impressive scene. We sat in silence, aware of the countless generations of Christians who had worshipped here, something that helped subdue the ego. After a while I walked through one of the arches that ran the length of the church, moving slowly to spend time before each of the icons. As I approached the corner of the building I noticed a small doorway where three old women were waiting to enter. As I drew nearer I could see past them to where many candles were casting a golden light across a small room. Once it was my turn to enter I was standing before a glass case around a silver box which contained the relics of Saint Demetrius. The woman in front of me was venerating them with great devotion, and so I took in the icons that surrounded me, the hands and faces appearing to have life as the candlelight moved with the flickering flames. I stepped forwards and crossed myself before kissing the glass and asking for his prayers. There were more visitors behind me and so I quickly moved aside. The cramped room meant we could only snatch a moment with the saint, but it was enough.

After Joseph had venerated Saint Demetrius we stood outside the church studying the map. Hagia Sophia was no more than ten minutes' walk away, and as we walked I explained some of its history. It was built in the eighth century on an even earlier site, and was designed after the Hagia Sophia in Constantinople. Arriving at the church we were first struck by the open lawned space that was the first green area we had seen in the city. The immediate impression of the church is, like that of the church of Saint Demetrius, one of great age. As we walked towards the arched entrance it created a mixture of feelings: that this was both a contemporary place of worship for a community alive today, but also of a historical monument that marked the ancient practices of people living centuries ago. This combination captured the reality of the Orthodox Church which continues to maintain and protect the traditions and faith of the first Christians.

Inside the church we found ourselves looking up into the dome which was covered with images of the Apostles and angels. Small arched windows were positioned near the top of the dome which created a crown of light above us. I was drawn towards the iconostasis which more than anything else communicated the great age and continuity of Orthodoxy. Once more we tried to take in as much as we could, but the impact of the light and colour was overwhelming. There were a number of groups being given tours of the church, and while this was going on individuals were quietly sitting or standing before icons, and everywhere the glow of candles was a visible manifestation of the inner prayers being offered.

Across the road from the church we found a small icon shop and in the window was Saint Paisios. I felt compelled to buy it, and was pleased to discover it was at a good price. As I handed over my cash the woman behind the counter said "Thank you Father." My beard had given me away and I was embarrassed not to be in my rassa. I resolved not to walk the streets improperly dressed again.

We strolled along the seafront towards the famous tower of Thessalonica, and got harassed by a group of young black men who smiled as they forcefully insisted we buy their wristbands. They had one tied around Joseph's wrist before he could refuse and then demanded money. Moored in the bay was a reproduction pirate ship which we decided to investigate. We discovered that it gave free twenty minute rides around the harbour which sounded too good to miss. It was only when Joseph bought drinks from the bar that we discovered how they could afford to give free trips: we nursed our coffees for the whole ride. Stepping off the boat we had well and truly become tourists, and in this frame of mind found a pleasant restaurant for lunch and spent the rest of the afternoon visiting the sites and taking photographs. Two or three more times Joseph brought up our visit to Saint Paisios, and I could sense how much it meant to him.

By the time we got back to the apartment the streets were busy with people returning from work and we felt very privileged to have so much free time. We sat and chatted on the balcony for an hour and Joseph disappeared to read. I wanted to check my emails and so headed back to the Dirty Duck to use their Wi-Fi. As I sat engrossed in my digital device a man in his mid-thirties entered and the barmaid must have told him I was English.

"What do you think of our city?" He called across to me.

"There are some beautiful churches," I said.

"You don't have churches like this in England."

"No," I agreed, "but we do have some good ones."

"Where else have you been visiting?"

"I've been to Mount Athos with my son."

"Athos!" he exclaimed, bringing his beer over from the bar to my table, "You are Orthodox?"

"Yes," I smiled.

His face lit up, "That is so good to hear."

"Have you been to Athos?"

"Yes, many times," he said, "but not for some years. I have a spiritual Father here in the city, so I do not need to visit the monks."

174

"Is he your priest?"

"Yes, such a man," he said, "he knows things before you say anything. In confession, if there is something I have forgotten he reminds me. He is a saint. God has given him many gifts to help the people here. This is what God does. In times like these he sends us saints to help us."

"We are visiting Saint Paisios tomorrow."

He shook his head, "No you will have to wait another day. The monastery is closed tomorrow."

My heart sank, "Why, what's happening?"

"Nothing, but it only opens to visitors every other day. You could have gone today."

I knew this was going to be a huge disappointment for Joseph, I took a sip of my drink. Seeing my reaction he said "Wait a moment, I have a friend who works there, I will check for you." He stood up and began tapping in the numbers. It was impossible to discern from his tone what his friend had said, but as he put his 'phone away he said "I am sorry, I asked if special arrangements could be made for you, but it is not possible. The nuns need time without visitors. How long are you staying in Thessaloniki?"

"Just tomorrow morning, we were hoping to visit the monastery on the way to our hotel. Thanks for trying for me."

"I am sorry for you, but you will have to come again. This is a good excuse for another trip." He grinned at the idea, and I smiled back. "My name is Andreas" he said, offering me his hand.

At that moment the right thing to do would have been to reveal I was a priest, but I didn't, I was still embarrassed not to be dressed properly. "Spyridon," I said. He didn't react to an Englishman having such a name and I assumed he thought it was my baptismal name.

Just then the barmaid switched on the television and Andreas swore under his breath. He pointed his finger at the screen and shouted something in Greek. The barmaid pulled a face and turned off the television. He looked at me with a serious expression, "My brother works on those things. He can fix any TV no matter what is wrong. But he says half of the electronics in them don't make sense, they don't have anything to do with making the picture or the sound. They put stuff in them to watch us, I really believe this."

I wasn't sure how to react, I shook my head and frowned, "Who do you think is behind this?"

"The United Nations," he said without hesitation, "they are killing my country, and they spy on everyone. We are at the end of time when they do such things." He could sense my reaction, "I know it sounds crazy to say such things," he said, "but I do not say this just because of the television. The devil is laughing now, but he won't be laughing for long."

"I agree, but the saints have warned us about what must happen before that time."

"Yes, and what they told us is already happening. There is going to be a war," said Andreas, "we must prepare ourselves for terrible things."

His eyes were calm and he spoke these last words in a sombre tone. It was a warning I was becoming familiar with and I didn't dismiss what he had to say. But on a day when I had been gallivanting around Thessalonica and taking boat rides, I was uncomfortable having to hear it. It was a relief to see Joseph enter the bar but I also knew I had to break the bad news to him. As he approached Andreas stood and said "I hope you enjoy the rest of your trip." I thanked him and Joseph sat down. The barmaid came over to our table and I ordered some drinks.

"We can't visit Saint Paisios tomorrow, the monastery is shut."

To my surprise Joseph took the news without any great reaction, "That's a real shame," he said, "what will we do instead?""

"We don't need to be at the hotel until the evening, we could have another day in Thessalonica."

"Fair enough," he said, "we could find some more of the churches."

His reaction lifted my spirits, and as I made the decision to wear my rassa for the rest of the trip, the barmaid brought us over another complimentary bowl of snacks. She gave Joseph a big smile as she placed them on the table, and I sensed she was interested in more than earning a tip.

Chapter 15

Now that we were confident with our directions we decided to spend our second day looking for more churches. The bus strike was ongoing so we walked at a leisurely pace through the streets. I was now dressed in my rassa, and as a result felt more comfortable. We decided to begin with another visit to Saint Demetrius' church so that Joseph could venerate his relics again. On our way in we were approached by a number of Romany women who pleaded for money. We gave them a little change but they persisted in begging for more. I reached into my pocket and the young woman in front of me held out her hands expectantly. I gave her the only thing I had with me which was a small laminated icon of Saint Spyridon (I always carried a few). I slipped it onto her hand and blessed her, and before she could register what had happened I was in the church.

I sat quietly while Joseph waited to speak to Saint Demetrius. I imagined the local priest whose served here and envied him a little. But then I remembered my small congregation back in England and knew I had more blessings than I deserved. When Joseph found me he said "Let's go back to Hagia Sophia as well." I had no objections and so we retraced our steps from the previous day. There were fewer people this time and everyone present seemed intent on praying. As I walked towards the iconostasis a woman appeared at my right and took hold of my arm. She was in her late fifties and had a wild look in her eyes. She began speaking very quickly in Greek, and when I explained that I was English she said "Come with me, please Father."

"Where, where do you want to go?"

"To Saint Theodora, please Father, you must ask her to pray for me."

I let her lead me to a hidden area to the side of the iconostasis where the relics of Saint Theodora were on display. The woman released me and held out her hands for a blessing. She began relating to me in her broken English personal details of her life, many of which were full of tragedy and pain. I listened carefully, blessed her and then prayed with her to Saint Theodora. I gave her my last icon card of Saint Spyridon and asked her to remember me in her prayers. She seemed overjoyed to receive the humble gift and I was deeply touched by her humility.

I left her and found Joseph, and as we walked out of church I described what had happened. Outside the door we met a priest with a small group of people. Without thinking I said "Hello Father,"

"Hello," the priest responded in an American accent.

"Where abouts in America are you from Father?"

"Alaska," he said, "and you?"

"We are from England. I have an icon of Saint Herman in our icon corner back home," I told him, "he is a great saint."

"This is my daughter and my father," he said, "he is also a priest." The older man nodded and smiled.

We chatted for a little while about where we had been and about the state of Orthodoxy in our respective homelands, and he described how they had driven from Italy and were heading back to the states in two days. One of the Romany women approached us again and the Alaskan priest forcefully waved her away. We wished each other well and Joseph and I found a bench to sit on to plan where we would head next. I scanned the map and found the church of Saint Panteleimon, and then traced the route back to where we were. It was a short distance away and once more we joined the crowded pavements and this time headed east.

On first impression we could see that the church looked very old, but we later discovered that though it was built in the thirteenth and fourteenth centuries, it was only dedicated to Saint Panteleimon after the Ottomans had been driven out. We were fortunate to find it open, since it is usually closed except on Sundays, and a woman at the door kindly directed us to his relics. Saint Panteleimon is a saint I often turn to, and to be close to his physical remains was a great blessing. Orthodoxy teaches that the link between the physical and non-physical parts of us is never broken, that we are single being made up of the two. To be close to a saint's earthly remains is to bring us closer to their presence before God, and the holiness of his presence was tangible. We remained there for a while, content to pray in the cool shadows of this ancient church. We recognise the brevity of our own earthly life in such places, and once more any anxieties that I had been carrying were put into perspective. The reality of our hearts touching Heaven is filled with peace, and I was reluctant to leave. But the woman at the door looked like she was wanting to lock up and we thanked her and left.

As we crossed town we found ourselves at Thessaloniki's large covered market and decided to see what was available. The stalls were selling pretty much what could be found in any British market, the main difference was the types and styles of goods. For example, the butcher sold cuts of meat that I didn't recognise, and there were tangles of long sausages that were unknown back home. The clothes had a distinctive look to them too, fashions and designs that no one in Britain was wearing. As we followed the labyrinth of narrow alleys we met a group of four clergymen in black. As they saw me they each bowed slightly holding their hand to their chest, and the oldest of the group began speaking in what I thought I recognised as Romanian.

"I am sorry Father," I said, "I am English."

There was a look of surprise on their faces and the oldest of them said "We are from Gura Humorului, this is Father George from Voronet Monastery." He waved his hand toward a man with a long black beard who bowed his head slightly once more.

There was little to add, and with warm smiles we said our goodbyes. As we continued to explore the market we felt a few drops of rain penetrating the canvas roof, and suddenly the heavens opened and a downpour began. Even along the covered walkways water began gushing from the ceiling and everyone around us rushed for shelter. Within thirty seconds a small river began flowing past us and the only dry places were inside the shops. We found a food stall with a large tarpaulin covering a couple of tables and chairs and decided to sit out the rain. At the counter I ordered two coffees and would have gladly paid the same price just for the shelter. As I sat down with Joseph Father George and one of the younger Romanian priests appeared and joined us out of the rain. The monk sat at our table, shaking some of the water from his rassa.

"So unexpected," he said.

"The sky was cloudless half an hour ago," I added.

"Yes, and it will be again soon," said Father George, "these storms come and go very quickly in Greece."

"Where are you heading?" I asked.

"We are on our way to the Holy Mountain."

"We have just been," I said.

"That is good," he looked at Joseph and then back at me, "it is important to introduce our sons to monastic life, but especially on the Holy Mountain."

"What is your monastery like in Romania?" Joseph said.

"It is very beautiful, God has blessed so many people through it, both monks and laity. But I may be moving to live on Mount Athos, I will be staying there a while to see if this is God's will."

"Why would you leave your monastery to go to Athos? Joseph asked.

"All monasteries bear witness to Christ, but especially the Holy Mountain. True theology finds its fulfilment in purity, not just personal purity, but purity of a way of life. Even in my own monastery I came to understand that the Holy Mountain offered something special which I must taste for myself."

"How is this purity different on Athos?" I said. "Couldn't you say this of all monasteries?"

"Yes, of course," said Father George, "every monk seeks to live as an offering to God. But on the Holy Mountain there is a life of repentance that is the true Christian life. Our Lord began His ministry by calling us to repent, and this is at the heart of the Holy Mountain. We can only repent when we see our sins, and life there enables monks to become truly aware of their sinfulness. But repentance requires trust in God's forgiveness, which is why there is joy in a monk's heart."

The priest joined us at the table, and Joseph and I turned and smiled, but Father George remained focussed on what he was saying. "We repent because we know that God's love for us is undeserved. We do not sit recounting sins from long ago, but in our hearts we know the depths of our sin and how God continues to love us. All Christians must long to respond to God's love as perfectly as they can, but we cannot. It is this pain that we find in our hearts, our inability to love God as he loves us. Too much Christianity in the West is presented as trying to be good, following ethical guidelines, and we see people turning away because it is not what their hearts need. Orthodoxy does not present a set of rules to follow, it provides us with the means to unite with God. There can be no hypocrisy when we are truly Christian because we know how deeply we have sinned against God's love, there is no pretence. In a monastery we reveal to our elder our inner thoughts, and so there can be no show of false goodness or virtue. Instead we are called to strive with our whole being for perfection, just as Christ called us to. Only in perfection can we love God as we should and find complete union with Him. The Holy Mountain is not full of saints, but the monks are seeking to be healed of their infirmities."

The priest said something in Romanian and Father George answered him and the two men nodded. The rain was continuing to fall and even the other café's table was now drenched. Joseph pulled his chair round as the puddles were splashing his way, and there was now no sign of any shoppers in the market. As the priest finished saying something to him, Father George turned back to us and said "Immanuel means "God with us", not a God to be shouted at from a distance, but

God Who enters our lives and makes Himself known. We are created to know God, not just believe in Him and think about Him. God revealed through Saint Gregory of the Holy Mountain that the divine energies are not created. When God's grace comes to us, it is not separate from God as the Roman Catholics and Protestants teach, but the uncreated light of God. But only when we are purified, washed clean of our passions, can we know this light. This is why we must repent, not because some ethical standard demands it, not because being good is our goal, but because only when we have overcome the passions can we enter complete union with God."

"But what about those of us who are not perfect?" Joseph asked.

"That is almost all of us," said Father George, "and in His compassion and love for us God still permits us to taste the sweetness of His presence. It is painful to know how generous God is to us when we see the truth of our hearts. But too many young people are not given the opportunity to seek God. If they are in the West they will be given a Christianity in name only, a matter of Bible readings and instructions about what they must not do in life. Who should wonder that their hearts seek something more? But not knowing how to do it they turn instead to pleasure, or drugs, or a million and one other things that materialism offers them. And then when they have exhausted these possibilities, and still their hearts are empty, they become depressed or even suicidal. No wonder!

Who could live such an empty life? It is a scandal that Christianity is presented in this way, stripped of its true purpose. The man-centred universe of the atheists has conquered western Christianity, turning it away from a life that is God-centred. So often it is evangelism and social action that western Christians see as their calling, they busy themselves with such things while their hearts do not have Christ. Of course there is an emotional or psychological attraction to God, and many western Christians are genuinely longing for Him. I have met many devout and pious Protestants who are sincere in their beliefs, but Christ has not moved from their mind to their heart. And what they mistake for the heart is sentimental feelings which make them feel good. Because it is how they feel that they make as the final arbiter of their experience. But let us never forget our calling is to carry a cross, not to find a way to make ourselves happy. Joy is deeper than human happiness because it comes from God, it is a gift to the human heart, not the product of human action."

The rain had begun to slow and the Romanian priest was peering at the clouds through a gap in the roof. I sensed our time with the monk was coming to an end, and so I asked him "Is there anything more than repent we can we do in the world to draw closer to God?"

"Yes, of course, we must try to remain conscious of God in whatever we are doing. The Jesus Prayer helps us in this, when we live and breathe only Christ we become sons of God. When God's grace works in us, we perceive the fullness of Orthodoxy for what it is and will not change even one dot. People in the world must guard themselves against heresy by preventing secular ways of life from converting them into secular people. It happens in small ways, attending parties in Advent, forgetting the saints and their holy days, all the little ways that the world wants to chip away at us until one day we are converted. It is up to us to convert the world. Not through clever arguments, but through the Orthodoxy of our lives. When light shines the darkness retreats. God's presence is a reality that human hearts recognise, but it must be authentic. And it can only be so when our own hearts are filled with Christ. We do not need to go knocking on doors like the Witnesses do, the whole world can be drawn into the Kingdom of God when the door is opened. We must build His Kingdom in our own hearts first. The world is in desperate need. During the enlightenment the West replaced God with man, but now man has failed and we see a rapid disintegration of the false kingdom. Who knows what kind of chaos will follow, what madness this will lead to. We must hold fast Father, now more than ever."

The priest was becoming restless, it was clear he couldn't follow everything the monk said in English. He got to his feet and said something to Father George who responded and then to us he said "We must find our companions, a blessing Father." He held his palms forward and I stood and blessed him. With that they turned and left, and Joseph said "Thank goodness for the rain."

It was late afternoon by the time we got back to the apartment and time to head to the hotel for our final night in Greece. We gathered our things and walked down to where there was a line of taxis on the main road. I leaned through the window of the first one and said "Hotel Avalon?"

"Yes," said the driver, and we climbed in. The interior was filthy, but the small icon cards stuck to his dashboard was reassuring. I tried to make conversation with him but his English wasn't good enough and I gave up. After ten minutes of driving we saw signs for the airport and I knew he was heading in the right direction. But after a while he turned off into a side street and did a U-turn. He pulled back out into the busy traffic and mumbled the hotel name under his breath. A few minutes later he pulled over once more and muttered to himself. I glanced over my shoulder at Joseph who clearly shared my concerns. All the time the meter was clicking over, and as the driver demonstrated further that he didn't know the way, what should have been a fifteen euro ride was now in the thirties.

"Don't you know where it is?" I said.

"Yes, don't worry about this," he waved at the meter, "I will find it."

After more running back and forth we all spotted a sign for the hotel and to our relief he followed the slip road up to the front doors. He charged us half of what the meter read and we watched as he drove into a dead end before reversing and eventually finding his way out of the hotel grounds.

The Avalon Hotel was where I had stayed on my last trip, I chose it because it was close to the airport and offered a free taxi service to guests who were catching a flight. It felt good to be somewhere familiar and I enjoyed being able to give Joseph the opportunity to stay at such a good hotel, even for one night. We had a room with a balcony and there was a relaxing sense of luxury. We decided our last meal in Greece should be a good one, and Joseph wanted to pay for it. The waiter brought us complimentary drinks, and it seemed the perfect way to end the trip. By the time we headed to bed our thoughts were turning to the aeroplane ride and seeing everyone at home, and I was beginning to feel my usual nerves about flying. The combination of the busy day, a big meal and alcohol meant we were asleep soon after getting into bed. But around three-thirty the telephone rang. I was still half asleep when I heard Joseph talking to someone. I checked the clock and was confused why someone would be ringing the room at this hour. Joseph hung up, "The flight's cancelled," he said.

I sat up, "What?"

"The hotel says that air traffic control has gone on strike. All flights are cancelled."

I hadn't fully come to, and immediately began cursing them. "What are we supposed to do now?" I shouted. "Did they say when the next flight will be?"

"No, they only rang up because William got in touch with them when he saw it on the news. Otherwise we wouldn't know."

I slumped back onto the bed, not sure what we would have to do. "I'll go online," I said, "maybe the air company website will have the information." The website revealed there wasn't another available flight for six days. I had a baptism booked for the following Sunday, and the parents had family members travelling from Bulgaria especially for the occasion. On top of all this I didn't know if I had enough money to pay for another six days of hotels. My early morning state of mind went into a panic, but there was nothing I could do to change our circumstances. I booked us in on the next flight and after more grumbling lay back in bed.

It was then that Joseph said "We'll be able to visit Saint Paisios now."

Chapter 16

Early the next morning I was online trying to find cheap hotels. Everything that looked reasonable was booked, and just as I was beginning to feel desperate I came across the Nea Metropolitan Hotel which claimed to be in the very heart of Thessaloniki. The price was very good, but they only had a room available for two days. I decided to book it and look for our next place later. I fired off a number of emails to my son William, pleading with him to call other priests near our parish to see if anyone could cover the baptism. But everyone back home was still sleeping because of the time difference and I got no response. Finally I went down to the desk at reception and booked us back in for what would be our last night; at least I hoped it would be. Unsure of how much money I would have left I asked for the cheapest accommodation they had, a basement level room without a balcony was available and I gladly took it.

With no flight to catch we spent the morning on the hotel's computer, they kindly printed off our new boarding passes for when we returned, and I sat grumbling at the prices of the city's hotels. Eventually William got back to me and assured me that Stephanie was going to try and find an available priest. This brought me a little comfort and I went for a short walk. Beyond the grounds of the hotel there was only scrub land, but I needed a few minutes to think things through. There was absolutely nothing I could do to change the situation, and worrying about the cost would only ruin the opportunity that had been given to us. By the time I returned to the room my mood had lifted. "You look a lot better," said Joseph.

"We might as well make the most of it and forget about the money."

"I already had," laughed Joseph, "I think another six days is great."

I managed to smile, "I agree."

We took a taxi back into Thessaloniki city centre and true to the website's claims, the hotel couldn't have been more central. It was basic but clean, just what we needed. Stepping out of the front door we were straight into the city action, and I was only sorry they didn't have any more days available. Before I could relax I was back on the internet looking for our next hotel, but there was nothing. We decided to eat lunch down on the sea front and found a friendly restaurant where everything tasted good. There were no other customers and again I wondered how these small businesses would survive. We did a little shopping, and with a room secured for two days relaxed and enjoyed being on holiday. We were greeted warmly by shop keepers, and when Joseph tried to buy an electrical adaptor for the Greek plugs we were given it as a gift. Whatever state the economy was in, there were still plenty of Greeks happy to welcome an English priest into their establishments with generosity.

Back at the hotel I immediately checked my emails and was assured that after spending the whole day making calls, my wonderful wife had sorted everything out. The mother of the child had accused me of deliberately orchestrating my extended stay, but apart from this the problem had been solved. Once more I realised I was only feeling stressed about the hotels because I had a fixed idea about what we should do. "What if we find somewhere outside Thessaloniki?" I said.

"As long as we visit Saint Paisios, I don't care where we end up."

I was grateful for his attitude, "Okay, I'll look for a hotel over that way."

Once I broadened my search there were lots of options, and we spent some time comparing photographs of different places, many of them at reasonable prices. Eventually we settled on a place across the bay, called Perea, the route would take us very close to the little town of Souroti where the monastery of Saint John the Theologian was located. I initially booked us in for one night, leaving us the option of moving on if we didn't like it, as there looked to be plenty of vacant rooms available.

The rest of our stay in Thessaloniki consisted of long walks exploring the noisy streets; we quickly became accustomed to city life and the time passed in a flash. The receptionist gave us directions to the nearest taxi rank and we set off with our bags. The first taxi driver shook his head when I gave him our destination, I couldn't tell if he had not heard of it or if he was unwilling to drive that far out from the city centre. But the next driver nodded confidently and invited us in. He was in his thirties with a good grasp of English, and as he weaved his way through the unruly traffic he asked us about our visit and what we thought of his country. Eventually I said "We want to visit Saint Paisios before we leave, is it far from our hotel?"

"No, it is very close, you will see signs for the monastery on the way." It was reassuring to hear this and when we spotted the signs we knew we could trust him. Once we had left the duel carriageways the scenery improved, we were driving through fields punctuated by isolated houses that all looked to have been built in the last five to ten years. It created a sense of impermanence to life, as though things had and were continuing to change quickly. Our hotel was at the end of an empty road where four similar hotels had been erected just a short walk from the beach. The name "Perea Hotel" was spelt out in huge letters across the building. As we pulled up the taxi driver handed me his business card, "When you want to leave, call me." After our previous experience he seemed like a good bet and I tucked the card away safely.

The hotel owner or manager, I was never sure which he was, sat at a table outside the hotel, a large overweight man who gave no sign of being pleased to see us. He gave a slight nod of the head as we approached but remained indifferent as we passed him. Inside we felt the impact of the air conditioning and a young woman behind the desk made more of an effort than we had been greeted with by her boss. She confirmed our details and led us down to our room on the ground floor. It was bigger and more luxurious than our last place, with a huge walk-in shower that would get a lot of use during our stay. I stepped out onto the balcony and seeing the perfect blue of the sea just across a field from us decided we had made a good choice. "I could stay here longer than one night," Joseph said.

"Shall I try and book us in for tomorrow as well?"

"Why not three days? We can visit Saint Paisios on the way back to the Avalon."

I went back down to the desk and the receptionist confirmed we could stay as long as we wanted. We unpacked and took a walk into town along the seafront. Waiters called out to us in the hope of seeing our money but we waved back to show we had other plans. We cut back into town and found a very large church. It was constructed of prefabricated concrete sections which didn't detract from how impressive it looked. Outside it a small brick structure was filled with icons and burning candles, and we paused to pray and add to the number of little flames. We chose to eat at a little side-street restaurant, and when I asked for non-meat food the waiter did his best to find something for us. In the end we settled on pittas stuffed with various vegetables which was as good as anything pictured on the menus. As we sat eating, two old men began looking our way and I wondered if it was the strange dishes we were consuming or our English voices. Seeing our soft drinks one of them called across to us "You should try the wine."

"Thank you," I said, "maybe tomorrow."

He came over to our table, he was struggling with his hip or leg and looked to be in pain. "I have lived in England, near London, but I prefer Greece."

"Are you Greek?" I asked.

"No, I am Swiss. I have lived in many places, but this is where I will now stay. The sunshine is good for me." He smiled, "and I like the wine. Is this your son?"

"Yes, Joseph. Do you have family here?"

"No, just my wife, our children live all across Europe, France, Norway and one is in England. It is the way of things today I suppose, but their mother misses them."

"It's the same in England, people are moving around much more even inside the country."

"It is a great worry to me, although I am a hypocrite because I enjoy travelling, and what should I do, expect my children to come with me? But still it worries me that families are broken up this way. We make different decisions in life when we are far from home. We act a certain way when everyone knows us, but when we are a stranger we create a different life for ourselves."

"Some people find that a good thing," I said, "a chance to reinvent themselves or leave things behind."

"Yes, I can understand that, but it is difficult to truly belong to a community that has no roots or long connection. And of course, there is no one noticing if you don't go to church."

"In England it is normal not to attend church, in fact people notice if you do."

"I am not a churchgoer myself, but I see the benefits for people, and I am envious of you having faith. At my age the door of death is already beginning to open. It is not easy to face such things without faith."

"Sadly too many people don't see the door opening soon enough. We are taught to avoid the subject, we look away. But the saints tell us to reflect on death every day. They say we cannot live properly if we do not understand our mortality."

"Yes," he nodded, "this is true. I have been a fool for much of my life, and only now do I have enough wisdom to regret it all. But regret isn't enough. It doesn't help us sleep at night."

"There is a peace that faith brings, but it isn't a way of avoiding the struggle of life. God makes demands on us, we are called to carry our cross."

"There are many different crosses, some we build ourselves and there is no resurrection on the other side. This is the foolishness that we bring on ourselves," he said.

"It's not too late to turn things around, Christ forgave the thief on the cross beside him. His way of life built that cross, but Christ promised resurrection."

"Yes, but perhaps I am like the other thief who also built his own cross and was unable to ask for His mercy."

"I don't think he was unable, only that he was unwilling."

The old man's head bobbed as he chuckled to himself, he raised his glass to us and swallowed the last of its contents. "I hope you have a safe journey home." He returned to his friend who refilled his glass. They resumed their conversation in Greek and we finished our vegetables.

Back at the hotel we sat on our balcony watching the aeroplanes landing at one end of the airport and taking off at the other. As the days passed we realised we would soon be sitting on one of them, and just as in Gatwick, it was comforting to see so many survive what was a commonplace event. From the beach we were able to look out across the bay back at Thessaloniki, surrounded by the low hills which we had ridden through to reach Athos. The sky was permanently cloudless, and our extra time in Greece had come to an end. On our final evening we packed and took down the small icon corner we had constructed, all except for Saint Paisios. We wanted him there with us even before we visited him.

Chapter 17

Wanting to avoid the queues we decided to leave for the monastery in Souroti as early as possible. Before sleeping I had fished out the taxi driver's card and he sounded happy to arrange the pickup. We ate breakfast in a deserted hotel restaurant during which I kept one eye on the clock. After grabbing our bags we went to reception where the manager was now standing for the first time since we arrived. He handed me a receipt and asked me to fill out an online questionnaire about our stay which I assured him I would, since we'd had a good experience. Outside the taxi was waiting for us and the driver smiled and waved as we approached. He helped throw our bags in the boot and we climbed in to a very warm car.

"How long do you think it will take to get there?" I asked.

"Oh, maybe fifteen minutes, it's not far."

I was pleased to have this confirmed, it meant we would arrive around half an hour before the monastery gates opened, which I assumed would enable us to beat the crowds. The roads were fairly busy as the commuters made their way into the city, but once we turned off towards Souroti we had the roads to ourselves. I had imagined a small village with a quaint monastery building perched in one corner, but the town was fairly developed, no doubt supported by the flow of pilgrims. At a sign we couldn't read but which was marked with a large Orthodox cross the driver pulled into a field and our hearts sank. There were at least half a dozen coaches parked and ten or so rows of cars, and around the gate was standing a small group of teenagers. Expecting the taxi to drop us off at the back of the queue I estimated it would be some time before we got in, but instead he drove past them all directly to the gate. Four stewards were directing traffic, and our driver exchanged a few words with them. The stewards wandered away and the driver turned to me and said "If you wait here at the gate they will give you a lift to the monastery."

I still wasn't sure what this would mean in turns of when, but I paid and thanked him. "Are there taxis available in town?"

"Don't worry, just ring me again and I'll come and pick you up. If I can't come I will send someone."

It all sounded reassuring and we thanked him again. As he drove back down the dusty road Joseph and I tried to guess where the back of the queue was, but one of the stewards approached us and waved us forwards. "Please Father, sit this side in the shade." Embarrassed to be given such preferential treatment we nonetheless gladly sat where he pointed, and the teenagers around us looked on without any resentment. Joseph leaned close to me and whispered "I'm glad I'm with a priest."

During the short wait more cars arrived, and the stewards loudly directed them into the field. Eventually four cars were driven to immediately outside the gates and we were invited over. "Get in Father, we will drive you up." As we were about to climb in the steward said "No, a car each." Joseph got into the one behind us, and a moment later the large wooden gates swung open. Ahead of us was a meandering road that the driver took at some speed. As we reached the car park outside the monastery I asked him how much he wanted and he said, "No father, this is a free service." As I pulled my bag out Joseph's car arrived beside us and there was no sign of anyone else coming. One of the stewards pointed us in the right direction and we entered the monastery through a large stone archway on either side of which were mosaics of saints in intensely bright colours. Beyond the wall it was possible to see the orange roofs of the monastery buildings, but only once we were beyond the gateway did its full size and beauty strike us. At the centre of the complex, as with all purpose built monasteries, was the church. This one dwarfed everything else, its high tiled towers topped with black crosses. Across the front of the church were a series or stone archways which broke the rigid shapes into geometric patterns. Every wall was carefully designed to incorporate layers of coloured stone between the bricks, and this communicated a sense that nothing had been built solely for utility: the beauty of the nuns' faith was reflected in their environment. As we followed the little path towards Saint Paisios' grave we could see out over a large plain that extended to hills in the distance. In the early morning sun it looked like paradise.

As we came around the side of the church we saw ahead of us a large wooden single-storey bell tower, and beyond this was a set of steps that took us into a flower garden. At the far end of this stood a grave marked with a simple cross. There were still no other visitors around and we approached slowly, gathering our thoughts. I found myself praying to him as I stepped closer and as we knelt beside the grave there was a sense of his presence as tangible as that of Joseph beside me. To be so aware of a saint's presence is a sweet experience, and I could sense myself feeling lighter, an internal lifting of any pressure or worries, it was the reality of his holiness.

I wasn't sure how long we prayed there but I became aware of people approaching down the path and so kissed the cross before they could see what I was doing. We stood and stepped back to let people through, and watched as they quickly knelt to pray before moving on. We followed after them and a nun directed us through the church. Amongst the shadows large icons met us and we venerated them as we moved before them. Sitting quietly in the dark were nuns bowed in prayer, and everyone passed through with great reverence. We purchased some candles and lit them before the Theotokos, and I was filled with gratitude for the opportunity to be so close to Saint Paisios.

Outside the church some cups were lined up beside a tap and the water from it was chilled and refreshing. A few cameras appeared despite the "No Photography" signs, and everyone began to visibly relax and chat. Joseph walked towards one of the walls to take in the view, and so I found some shade and sat on a wooden bench to sip my drink. From a doorway to my left an elderly nun appeared and came straight to me. "A blessing Father."

I stood and blessed her, and she indicated for me to sit. She sat beside me, and looked at me with dark eyes full of gentleness. In a soft Greek accent she said "You have visited the saint?"

"Yes, we feel blessed to be here, I've come with my son."

"Saint Paisios was seen by many people to have a simplicity about him, but in truth everything he did was theological. Do you know what I mean by that?"

I shook my head, "I'm not sure."

"He lived every moment focussed on God, this is theological. God was the centre of everything for him, and so even in small things eternity was present with him. His simplicity was freedom, the freedom that we were created to live. God's image was restored in him so that he knew something of the freedom of this image. When our nature is free, we become Christ-like. It takes great struggle and self-sacrifice to achieve this condition, but Saint Paisios was so grace-filled that his efforts were rewarded. In the saints is a great mystery, it is

God's revelation to us of the way we were before the fall. If we come to know the life of a saint we glimpse something of the true nature of man, uncluttered; the saints are man's offering to God, but also a gift from God to us."

She turned and her gaze seemed to penetrate me, but there was nothing to fear, in her look was only compassion. "When we receive Christ in Holy Communion, we are drawn deeper towards this great mystery. God offers us union with Him, the union we turned our backs on, but despite our sin God does not fail to love us. Christ came to earth, He left the company of angels to walk with us in our misery, but in doing so He transformed our pain to joy, destroyed death with life. And still He offers Himself to us, again and again from the altar, so that we may draw closer to Heaven."

She spoke quietly but firmly, and as I listened I lost all awareness of the growing numbers of people that were coming out of the church. "I must organise the cups," she said, and without another word walked over to the tap. Joseph was standing watching from a small distance away, not wanting to interrupt her. I went over to him and smiled, there was no need to say anything.

We walked back to where the stewards had dropped us off and found the car park full. Crowds were still heading towards the monastery and the impact Saint Paisios has had and is having on the world was very clear. As we contemplated which route would get us quickest past all the cars the steward who had earlier driven me up the hill called out to us from the shade of a wall where he was sharing a cigarette with the others: "Father, Father."

I turned to see him approaching, hoping he was about to offer to drive us back down the hill. But he had something better in mind. "Father, where are you going?"

"Back into town, we need to find a taxi to our hotel."

"Which hotel?"

"Avalon," I said.

"Wait here a moment," and with that he strode confidently towards the visitors getting into their cars to leave. He exchanged a few words with a man, and we watched as he then began talking to a young couple. He pointed back at us and I saw the young man nodding. The steward waved us over, "Father, they will give you a lift to your hotel." I wasn't sure who to thank first, the young man smiled as he pulled his seat forward to let us in. As I began to follow Joseph in the man stopped me,

"Please Father, sit in the front."

I was a little embarrassed to watch the woman, who looked to be in her early twenties, climbing in to the back seat beside Joseph, but they were insistent. They assured us that their journey took them very near to our hotel, which relaxed me a little, and we settled in to a comfortable journey.

"How often do you come to visit Saint Paisios?" I asked.

"Not very often," said our driver, "but we are getting married in a few months, and wanted to ask him to pray for us." It was encouraging to see such simple and honest faith in people their age, and it seemed a natural thing for them to do in an Orthodox culture.

The sign for the hotel we had seen five days earlier with our incompetent taxi driver announced our arrival and as we drew up outside the reception doors we thanked them for their kindness. After pulling my seat forward to let Joseph out he asked for a blessing. I prayed for their future together, and with an exchange of warm smiles he slid back into his seat and drove away. With a sense of déjà vu we entered the air conditioned luxury of the hotel and introduced ourselves to the receptionist.

"I am sorry Father, your room is not available for another two hours. You are welcome to relax here until then." She pointed to the comfortable leather couches which at any other time would have been very enticing, but we were keen to settle into our own private space and talk.

"Are there any other rooms available?" Joseph asked.

"Only the rooms with balconies on the upper floor."

Joseph looked at me, "I'll pay the difference if you fancy it."

I didn't hesitate, and we were soon sliding the electronic door pass through its slot to our room. Having believed our last night here was our final night, there was an odd sense to returning and doing it all again. But determined to make a night of it, we ate and drank too much, and ended the evening sitting on our balcony drinking wine. The additional six days had been a tremendous blessing, not only because we had visited the saint, but that it had given us a chance to spend so much time together at a time in Joseph's life where we would probably never have the opportunity again.

The sky was overcast, and as we sat talking the clouds grew darker. Around nine o'clock intense forked lightning began snaking from the sky, and the whole of Thessaloniki seemed to rumble with the thunder. "There's no way anything will be taking off from the airport in this," I observed with a little concern.

"Don't worry, it'll have passed by morning."
Large raindrops began spotting the street beneath us, and a number of sparrows sought shelter with us under our roofed balcony. They began to fly back and forth along the length of the building as the rain grew heavier. I have no enthusiasm for flying at the best of times, but now my imagination was conjuring up wet runways and strong winds. Eventually the rain grew so heavy that we had to retreat into the room, and sitting on our beds we chatted until late, neither of us wanting to let go of our last day there.

Chapter 18

By the following morning the clouds had moved on leaving us the usual cloudless, blue sky. I was up early and entered an empty restaurant for breakfast. The waitress on duty bravely managed to smile and maintain her polite demeanour even at this hour, and when I asked if she minded if I took my food out by the pool she said "Of course," and held the door open for me. I was half way through my food when Joseph appeared with his plate to join me. "The food here is too good," he laughed.

"I know, if we stayed too long we'd be twice our size."

The air was warm and still, and we took it in turns to fetch coffee refills. But eventually we knew we had to bring it to an end, and we went back to our room to finally pack away for the return home. We waited on those leather sofas for the hotel's free taxi service, and I realised how different Joseph was from myself at his age. I had only been a Christian for three or four years, but here he was, an Orthodox man returning from Mount Athos. He had a head start on me. I had had to convert to Orthodoxy, he knew nothing else.

The short drive back to the airport brought us back to reality, Thessaloniki airport was chaotic and noisy. We passed through security with my usual body search and joined the crowds of mainly English holiday makers facing a return to their jobs and ordinary lives. After a couple of hours the gates opened for our flight and we moved forwards and out into the sunshine to ride the airport bus out to our waiting aeroplane. During the flight we barely spoke, both deeply immersed in our books and our own thoughts. Joseph called me over to the window to watch the Alps passing beneath us again, their snow-covered peaks merging into the white cloud above them. Eventually the pilot announced we were approaching England, and once we were over the Channel the ground turned a deep green. It was comforting to see how beautiful England is, and we were glad to be home.

But there was a final surprise. Too many aeroplanes were wanting to land at once and the pilot informed us that we would have to go into a holding pattern until a space was made available for us to land. The left side of the aeroplane suddenly dipped so that only the ground could be seen. Through the windows on the other side of us there was now only sky, punctuated by the glimpse of other aeroplanes making the same manoeuvre. Eventually the pilot righted us and we came in over London. We hit a lot of turbulence and I could see concern on Joseph's face. I looked instinctively at the stewards who were happily chatting in their seats and took the reassurance I wanted from it.

With so many flights arriving at once there was a sudden back-log of passengers for customs to deal with. An enormous queue zig-zagged through the airport, and without fail, one of the customs officers headed straight for me. "Are you a UK citizen?"

The question was put to me in an East-European accent, and so, in my most received pronunciation I said "I most certainly am." I caught Joseph's eye and knew exactly how he would react.

With the excitement of a pilgrimage no longer ahead of us, the train ride home dragged a little, and with twice as much time spent on British trains than we had in the air, we eventually made it home. There were lots of stories to tell, and lots of questions to answer. We looked at photographs on the computer and accepted that we really were back. But a pilgrimage to Mount Athos is not something that can be summed up like other trips, and its meaning isn't immediately apparent. Now that a few months have passed, I am occasionally caught by surprise when something small will trigger a memory. But more than anything, I find myself remembering that Sunday morning at Gregoriou Monastery when I prepare for Divine Liturgy. If I am tired or distracted by some small problem, I remind myself that we are linked to the monks and pilgrims on the Holy Mountain, and to all Orthodox Christians around the world. The reality of joy is never far away, and its depths are experienced most acutely when it is found at the heart of struggle.

Printed in the USA
CPSIA information can be obtained
at www.ICGtesting.com
CBHW031929090824
12961CB00009B/319